200 Italian favorites

200 Italian favorites

hamlyn **all color**

Marina Filippelli

An Hachette UK Company
www.hachette.co.uk

First published in Great Britain in 2009 by Hamlyn,
a division of Octopus Publishing Group Ltd
2–4 Heron Quays, London E14 4JP
www.octopusbooksusa.com

Copyright © Octopus Publishing Group Ltd 2010

Distributed in the U.S. and Canada by Octopus Books USA:
c/o Hachette Book Group
237 Park Avenue
New York NY 10017

Some of the recipes in this book have previously appeared
in other books published by Hamlyn.

ISBN: 978-0-600-62090-7

Printed and bound in China

1 2 3 4 5 6 7 8 9 10

Standard level spoon measurements are used in all recipes.

Ovens should be preheated to the specified temperature
—if using a fan-assisted oven, follow the manufacturer's
instructions for adjusting the time and the temperature.

Fresh herbs should be used unless otherwise stated.

Medium eggs should be used unless otherwise stated.

The Food and Drug Administration advises that eggs should
not be consumed raw. This book contains some dishes made
with raw or lightly cooked eggs. It is prudent for vulnerable
people such as pregnant and nursing mothers, invalids, the
elderly, babies, and young children to avoid uncooked or lightly
cooked dishes made with eggs. Once prepared, these dishes
should be kept refrigerated and used promptly.

This book includes dishes made with nuts and nut derivatives.
It is advisable for those with known allergic reactions to nuts
and nut derivatives and those who may be potentially
vulnerable to these allergies, such as pregnant and nursing
mothers, invalids, the elderly, babies, and children, to avoid
dishes made with nuts and nut oils. It is also prudent to check
the labels of pre-prepared ingredients for the possible inclusion
of nut derivatives.

contents

introduction

introduction

Italian food is now so popular that classics such as lasagna or tiramisu have become household favorites in all corners of the world. Fuss-free homely food, fresh ingredients, and simple techniques all make for a cuisine that has instant appeal to the modern cook. Anybody can cook Italian, and whether you are throwing together a quick pasta dish or letting a stew slowly simmer on the stovetop, the beauty of Italian cooking is that most dishes don't demand a lot of preparation time. For this reason, having a good repertoire of dishes to hand can be a lifesaver for busy weekday family meals and for entertaining alike.

eating the Italian way

Italians love their food so much that the dining table is the hub of the family. Breakfast generally consists of a cappuccino or espresso with cookies or a *brioche*, which in Italy is more like a croissant. Lunch and dinner are not dissimilar in their structure. Traditionally, they are split into four courses: *antipasto*, *primo piatto*, *secondo piatto* and the *dolce*. The *antipasto* (appetizer) can be either one dish or a combination of several small dishes, served tapas-style and referred to in the plural as *antipasti*. Then comes the *primo piatto* (first course), which may be pasta, soup, risotto, or polenta, depending on personal and regional preferences. The *secondo piatto* (second course) is a meat or fish dish

accompanied by vegetables or salad. Finally comes the *dolce* (dessert), which is hardly ever skipped but often only consists of a simple fruit salad or a bowl of fruit taken to the table for everyone to tuck into. Bread and wine are a constant at the Italian table and most people complete their meal with a shot of espresso.

Nowadays, not all Italian meals consist of so many courses. Frequently, just a pasta and a meat dish are served, followed by a fruit, or a bowl of pasta, then a vegetable side dish. A heavy lunch could be followed by just a wholesome soup, such as minestrone, for dinner. Whatever the meal, however, it is unlikely that an Italian will ever leave the table having eaten only a huge bowl of pasta or a large steak—that just wouldn't constitute a properly balanced meal and they have too healthy a relationship with food for that.

regional favorites

Italians often argue that there is no such thing as Italian food but rather lots of regional culinary traditions. Fresh pasta, for instance, is a northern dish and is hardly ever eaten in southern Italy. In the south, cooks exclusively use olive oil, while in the first half of the 20th century butter was the cooking medium of choice in the north. The divisions used to be distinct: pizza, tomatoes, mozzarella cheese, and chili belonged to the south, while risotto, cream, and black pepper were essentially northern. Today, the borders are blurred and favorite regional ingredients and dishes have become popular throughout the country and

beyond. The recipes in this book represent family favorites from all over the country. Most are traditional, while some are inspired by contemporary flavor combinations.

the Italian pantry

The Italian cook depends on a well-stocked pantry. Most of these ingredients are available in supermarkets, with only the more unusual ones requiring a trip to an Italian deli.

anchovies

Most commonly used in southern cooking, anchovies can be bought fresh or preserved in salt or oil. Salted anchovies taste fresher than those preserved in oil, but will need thorough rinsing to remove the salt. The flavor and saltiness of preserved anchovies can be mellowed by soaking them in milk. The recipes here use the preserved fish.

capers

These small flower buds are preserved in salt or brine. Rinse thoroughly in cold water to remove the saltiness or sharpness from the vinegar before using. Small capers are generally more flavorsome than larger buds.

cheeses

Mozzarella This can be made from cows' milk or water buffaloes' milk (*mozzarella di bufala*). Cows' milk mozzarella is more than adequate to use in cooking when it is going to be melted, but if you are planning to eat your mozzarella fresh, for instance in a tomato and mozzarella salad, it is worth splashing out on buffalo mozzarella, which tastes creamier. Only buy mozzarella kept in water.

Parmesan *Parmigiano Reggiano* is a cows' milk cheese made in the Emilia-Romagna region of northern Italy. It is used extensively, grated onto pasta, stirred into risottos, or shaved onto salads. It is also delicious broken into small pieces and eaten as a nibble with a glass of red wine. *Grana Padano* is similar to Parmesan and makes a more economical choice for use in cooking.

Pecorino This sheep's milk cheese is made in central and southern Italy. There are different varieties, which can be aged until they are ready for the table or matured further until dry and crumbly, to be used grated in cooking.

Ricotta This is a naturally low-fat soft cheese made from the whey left over from cheese making. The whey is reheated, then strained into baskets to drain, hence the name *ricotta*, which literally means "recooked." The most commonly found ricotta outside Italy is made from cows' milk and it is the one recommended for the recipes in this book.

Fontina This is a mild cheese from Piedmont, which melts evenly and smoothly, making it perfect for cooking. You can find it in good supermarkets and delis.

Gorgonzola and dolcelatte Both these blue cheeses are often used in pasta sauces. Gorgonzola is the strongest, comparable to Stilton or Roquefort. Dolcelatte is much creamier, with a milder, more delicate flavor.
Mascarpone A full-fat, very thick cream cheese with a rich, smooth texture and mild flavor, which is famously used in the classic dessert, tiramisu.

hams

Prosciutto is the generic Italian word for ham. *Prosciutto crudo* (literally meaning "raw ham") is the most commonly known Italian ham, of which the most famous variety is *Prosciutto di Parma*. It is a raw ham cured in salt, then hung to dry and age. What makes it so special is that it is made with the hind legs of pigs fed on the whey left over from producing Parmesan cheese, making it sweeter than other *prosciutti crudi*. *Prosciutto cotto* is cooked ham. Speck, a smoke-cured ham from the northern borders of Italy, is also used in some of the recipes. It has a robust, smoky flavor and can be found in most delis and supermarkets. Westphalian ham can be used as an alternative.

olive oil

There are different grades of olive oil. Extra virgin olive oil is made from the first cold pressing of olives and its rich flavor can vary from peppery to nutty or grassy. For best results, it is essential to use extra virgin in recipes where the oil is not cooked or where it features as one of the main ingredients.

Regular, commercially produced and less expensive olive oil can be used in recipes where the oil is used for frying or sautéing vegetables at the beginning of cooking.

pasta

Pasta is eaten throughout Italy, with different regions favoring different shapes and sauces. It can be made with or without egg, using durum wheat and/or soft wheat flour and eaten fresh or dried. Italians have strong opinions regarding which pasta to use with which sauce, and there are many exceptions to the general rule. Your best guide to making the appropriate choice is tradition, so go with what recipes suggest and what you see being used in restaurants in Italy. Buy the best you can afford and choose authentic Italian brands.

People often hold the misconception that fresh pasta is superior or somehow more sophisticated than dried pasta. This couldn't be further from the truth. Fresh pasta is reserved for specific shapes and sauces and is most frequently eaten in central and northern Italy. In certain regions of southern Italy, such as the island of Sicily, people who eat pasta every day might never even have tasted it fresh!

polenta

This coarsely ground corn flour is cooked in water to the consistency of mashed potatoes and served with meat or squid in a sauce. Once cold, soft polenta sets into a rigid block that can be topped with other ingredients and broiled. It takes about 40 minutes to cook polenta, but you can get very good results with the instant polenta most Italians use in everyday cooking. It takes just five minutes to cook instant polenta, and therefore is the favored variety for the recipes in this book.

legumes

Cranberry beans, cannellini beans, chickpeas, and lentils are very popular in Italian soups, stews, and salads. Beans and chickpeas are eaten fresh when in season, but when cooking them from dry, they will need soaking overnight in cold water. Canned beans, rinsed, can be used if time is short. You will need twice the quantity of canned beans to dried, so if a recipe calls for $\frac{1}{2}$ cup dried cranberry beans, for example, use 1 cup rinsed canned cranberry beans. Italians often save time by cooking with canned beans and as a result their brands are generally of an outstanding quality, so are well worth searching out.

risotto rice

This is now readily available in supermarkets and delis, so there is no need to attempt making risotto with any other rice. Avoid generically labeled risotto rice and opt instead for one of three specific varieties grown in the Po Valley: arborio, carnaroli, and vialone nano. Stirring risotto as it cooks helps the grains release their starch and it is this stirring that makes the final result so creamy.

tomatoes

There is an abundance of tomatoes of every different kind available in Italy in summer, from juicy plum tomatoes to sweet cherry tomatoes and green salad tomatoes. Each variety has its own use, and San Marzano plum tomatoes are prized for making sauces. These are the tomatoes most commonly used peeled in cans, chopped or whole. Good-quality canned tomatoes should not be frowned upon and Italians happily use them in winter to make their sauces. In fact, you are better off using canned tomatoes than unripened acidic greenhouse tomatoes any day! Passata is smooth, raw pureed tomatoes sold bottled or in cartons to use in cooking.

mushrooms

The most widely available wild mushrooms in Italy are porcini, chanterelles, and girolles. During their short season in late summer and fall, they are eaten raw in salads, pan-fried with garlic and stirred into pasta, eaten on *bruschette* or polenta, used in risottos, or served with sliced steak. Any other time of the year, Italians rely on dried mushrooms that need soaking in hot water before cooking. Of these, porcini are the most popular, stirred into stews, soups, and risottos, and delicious pan-fried with the most mundane field mushrooms. Make sure you use the soaking water from mushrooms, as it is packed with flavor.

vinegar

Red wine vinegar is the most commonly used vinegar for both dressing salads and cooking. Balsamic vinegar, made in Modena, is also popular but it is only really worth buying good-quality aged balsamic that should be rich, sweet, and syrupy. The real thing can be very pricey, but a little goes a long way with balsamic vinegar and just a few drops are enough to enliven a salad, sauce, or even a bowl of fresh strawberries.

recommended equipment

All the recipes in this book are technically quite straightforward, so don't call for very specialized equipment. A well-stocked kitchen with cutting boards, sharp knives, and a range of different size pans and baking pans is all you'll need, while the list below suggests a few useful extras.

large saucepan

You cannot cook pasta properly in a small saucepan. You will need a pan large enough so that the pasta has plenty of space to move around in the boiling water while cooking, to avoid it sticking to the base of the pan.

colander

Once your pasta has been cooked until tender but still firm to the bite, or *al dente*, you need to drain it very quickly. For this purpose, a large colander that you can sit in your sink is much more efficient than a sieve.

tongs

These useful utensils make it easy to serve long pasta such as spaghetti or linguine or to toss it into a sauce. They are also great for turning over meats or vegetables when frying or griddling.

nonstick skillet

This is not strictly essential but can be extremely helpful when trying to cut down on the quantity of oil or butter used in cooking. The best skillets have a heavy base and a solid, ovenproof handle.

ridged griddle pan

Griddling is a great way of cooking steaks, chops, chicken breasts, chunky fish steaks, and vegetables without the need for oil. The pan needs to be heated until smoking hot to sear the ingredients quickly and achieve the desired charred flavor and griddle marks.

mouli or ricer

One or other of these items is essential for achieving the light, fluffy, lump-free mash needed for gnocchi. Even if you don't make gnocchi very often, these cheap tools can be used for any recipe where ingredients need to be mashed.

techniques

Most of the techniques used are explained clearly in the relevant recipes in the book. However, to avoid unnecessary repetition in the many recipes for shellfish and seafood, here are some basic instructions on how to prepare them for cooking:

cleaning mussels

Scrub mussels under cold running water. Pull away the "beards" and discard any open shells that are broken or any that remain open when tapped. Soak in plenty of cold water for 30 minutes, then drain and rinse again in cold running water. Put in a bowl, cover with a wet dish towel, and keep refrigerated until needed.

cleaning clams

Wash the clams under cold running water, discarding any that are broken or that remain open when tapped. Soak in plenty of cold water for 30 minutes, then drain and rinse them again in cold running water. Place in a bowl, cover with a wet dish towel, and keep refrigerated until needed.

cleaning squid

Wash the squid under cold running water. Pull the tentacles away from the body. The squid's entrails will come out easily. Remove the clear piece of cartilage inside the body cavity and discard. Wash the body thoroughly, pulling away the pinkish membrane. Cut between the tentacles and head, discarding the head and entrails. Most fish merchants will be happy to take care of this messy job for you.

basic pizza dough

Makes **4**

Preparation time **15 minutes**, plus rising

¼ oz **fresh yeast** or
  1 teaspoon **quick-rising active dry yeast**
pinch of **superfine sugar**
4 cups **all-purpose flour**, plus extra for dusting
1½ cups **warm water**
1½ teaspoons **salt**

Dissolve the yeast in a bowl with the sugar, 2 tablespoons of the flour, and 3 tablespoons of the measurement water. Allow to stand for 5 minutes until the mixture starts to form bubbles, then add the remaining water. Add the salt and half the remaining flour and stir with one hand until you have a paste-like mixture. Gradually add all the remaining flour, working the mixture until you have a moist dough.

Shape the dough into a ball, cover with a moist cloth, and allow to rest in a warm place for 5 minutes.

Lightly dust a work surface with flour and knead the dough for 10 minutes until smooth and elastic. Shape into 4 equal-size balls and place, spaced apart, on a lightly oiled baking sheet. Cover with a moist cloth and allow to rise in a warm place for 1 hour. Use according to the particular recipe.

antipasti
& salads

fried vegetables in batter

Serves **6**
Preparation time **15 minutes**
Cooking time **15 minutes**

4 oz **cauliflower**
4 oz **broccoli**
1 **red bell pepper**
1 **zucchini**
1 **onion**
¾ cup **all-purpose flour**,
    for dusting
sunflower oil, for deep-frying
6 **flat-leaf parsley sprigs**
salt and **pepper**

Batter
2 **eggs**, lightly beaten
1 tablespoon **olive oil**
1¼ cups **chilled beer**
pinch of **salt**
2 cups **all-purpose flour**,
    sifted

Combine all the ingredients for the batter in a large bowl, mixing well but not worrying about any lumps that may have formed. Cover and chill while you prepare the vegetables.

Cut the cauliflower and broccoli into small florets. Core and seed the pepper, then cut it lengthwise into 8 strips. Slice the zucchini into ½ inch rounds and cut the onion into 8 wedges. Tip the flour into a bowl and season with salt and pepper, then toss in the prepared vegetables.

Heat enough oil for deep-frying in a deep saucepan to 350–375°F, or until a cube of bread browns in 30 seconds. Take 5 or 6 vegetable pieces from the flour, shake off any excess, then plunge into the batter. Lift out, letting the batter drip off slightly, then carefully plunge into the hot oil. Cook for about 3 minutes until golden. Remove with a slotted spoon and drain on paper towels. Once all the vegetables are cooked, lightly dust the parsley sprigs with flour, dip in the batter, and cook for 1–2 minutes, or until just golden.

Season the vegetables and parsley with salt and serve immediately.

For basil & lemon batter, make the batter as above, but add the grated zest of 1 lemon and 3 tablespoons chopped basil. Cover and leave to infuse in the refrigerator for at least 30 minutes before using as above. The parsley sprigs can be replaced with 8 drained anchovy fillets in olive oil.

porcini bruschetta with truffle oil

Serves **4**
Preparation time **10 minutes**
Cooking time **5 minutes**

4 thick slices of **country bread**
2 **garlic cloves**, bruised
extra virgin olive oil, for
    drizzling
2 tablespoons chopped **flat-
    leaf parsley**, plus extra to
    garnish
4 small **fresh porcini (ceps)**
lemon juice, for drizzling
truffle oil, for drizzling
salt and **pepper**

Toast the bread slices on both sides under a preheated medium broiler or in a preheated ridged griddle pan or over a barbecue. Rub 1 side of each toasted slice with the bruised garlic, then drizzle with the oil and sprinkle with the parsley.

Pick over the porcini and brush off any grit. Remove the stalks and thinly slice. Slice the caps as thinly as possible.

Cut the toasted slices in half. Sprinkle with the sliced porcini stalks, drizzle with a little lemon juice, and season with salt and pepper. Cover with the sliced porcini caps. Drizzle with more lemon juice and a little truffle oil, season again with pepper, and garnish with a little chopped parsley. Serve immediately.

For Parmesan, porcini, & radicchio bruschetta, prepare the bruschetta as above, omitting the parsley and lemon and dividing a handful of shredded radicchio leaves between each bread slice before adding the mushrooms. Top each bruschetta with a couple of Parmesan shavings, season with salt and pepper, and drizzle with extra virgin olive oil instead of the truffle oil.

arugula & garlic crumbed mussels

Serves **4**
Preparation time **15 minutes**
Cooking time **10 minutes**

½ cup **wild arugula leaves**
1 **garlic clove**
1 cup **fresh white bread crumbs**
4 tablespoons **extra virgin olive oil**
2 lb **mussels**, cleaned (see page 14)
salt and **pepper**
lemon wedges, to serve

Process the arugula and garlic in a food processor until roughly chopped. Add the bread crumbs and pulse until combined, then stir in the oil. Season with salt and pepper. Cover and chill until needed.

Put the mussels in a large saucepan with a tight-fitting lid and add water to a depth of 1 inch. Cover and bring to a boil over a high heat. Cook the mussels, shaking the pan frequently, for 2–3 minutes, or until the shells have opened. Drain, discarding any that remain closed. Pull away and discard the empty shell halves, reserving only the halves with the mussels attached.

Place the mussels, flesh-side up, on a baking sheet. Divide the bread crumb topping between the mussels and cook on the top shelf of a preheated high broiler for 1–2 minutes until the bread crumbs are golden. Serve immediately with lemon wedges on the side.

For tomato & parsley crumbed scallops, make the bread crumb mixture as above, but replace the arugula with ½ cup flat-leaf parsley and 4 drained sundried tomatoes in oil. Instead of the mussels, use 12 opened scallops. Loosen the scallops from their base shell by cutting through the muscle that attaches them to the shell with a small, sharp knife. Divide the bread crumb topping between the scallops and cook under the broiler as above, but increase the cooking time to 2–3 minutes.

fava bean bruschetta

Serves **4**
Preparation time **15 minutes**
Cooking time **3 minutes**

5 tablespoons **extra virgin
  olive oil**, plus extra for
  drizzling
2 **garlic cloves**, 1 crushed
  and 1 left whole
pinch of **dried red pepper
  flakes**
handful of **mint leaves**
1½ cups shelled **fava beans**,
  thawed if frozen, skins
  removed
1½ oz **Pecorino cheese**,
  grated
1 small **ciabatta loaf**, cut into
  8 thin slices
salt and **pepper**
Parmesan cheese shavings,
  to serve

Combine the oil, crushed garlic, pepper flakes, and mint in a bowl and allow to infuse for 10 minutes.

Meanwhile, lightly crush the fava beans in a separate bowl with a fork. Season with salt and pepper, then toss into the oil mixture with the Pecorino. Toast the bread slices on both sides under a preheated medium broiler or in a preheated ridged griddle pan or over a barbecue.

Rub the toasted slices with the remaining garlic. Top with the fava bean mixture and drizzle over a little oil. Sprinkle with Parmesan shavings and serve immediately.

For Parmesan & cannellini bean bruschetta,
combine 2 crushed garlic cloves, 1 teaspoon chopped rosemary, and 4 tablespoons extra virgin olive oil in a bowl and allow to infuse for 10 minutes. Drain a 13 oz can cannellini beans, rinse, then drain again. Lightly crush with a fork and stir into the oil mixture with 2 tablespoons freshly grated Parmesan cheese, salt to taste, and a large pinch of dried red pepper flakes. Serve on toasted bread slices, as above, drizzled with a little extra oil and sprinkled with Parmesan shavings.

carpaccio of fresh tuna

Serves **4**
Preparation time **10 minutes**,
  plus freezing

8 oz piece of **tuna loin**
juice of **3 lemons**
⅔ cup **extra virgin olive oil**
1 **garlic clove**, finely chopped
1 tablespoon **salted capers**,
  rinsed
2½ cups **wild arugula leaves**
salt and **pepper**
Parmesan cheese shavings,
  to serve

Trim the tuna of any membrane or gristle. Wrap tightly in plastic wrap and put in the freezer for about 1 hour until just frozen but not rock solid.

Meanwhile, beat together the lemon juice, oil, garlic, and capers in a bowl. Add salt and pepper to taste and beat until emulsified.

Unwrap the tuna and thinly slice with a sharp, thin-bladed knife. Arrange the slices on 4 large serving plates. Spoon the dressing over the tuna. Top with a tangle of arugula leaves and sprinkle with Parmesan shavings.

For fresh swordfish carpaccio, replace the tuna with 8 oz piece of swordfish. Freeze, thinly slice, and arrange on plates as above. Beat together the lemon juice, olive oil, and garlic, also adding 2 tablespoons chopped flat-leaf parsley, instead of the capers. Spoon over the plated fish and top with the arugula. Omit the Parmesan cheese.

balsamic figs with prosciutto

Serves **4**
Preparation time **5 minutes**
Cooking time **4–5 minutes**

8 **ripe fresh figs**
2 tablespoons **balsamic vinegar**
extra virgin olive oil, for drizzling
12 slices of **prosciutto**
1¼ cups **wild arugula leaves**
salt and **pepper**

Cut the figs in half and arrange, cut-side up, on a baking sheet. Brush with the vinegar and lightly drizzle with oil. Season with a little salt and a generous grinding of pepper.

Cook under a preheated high broiler for 4–5 minutes until heated through and a little charred.

Arrange 3 slices of prosciutto on each serving plate. Top with the broiled figs and sprinkle with arugula leaves. Drizzle over a little more oil and serve while the figs are still warm.

For minted melon with prosciutto, put a sliced small, ripe melon on a platter with 12 slices of prosciutto, then give this simple, classic Italian *antipasto* a modern twist by sprinkling it with 5 torn mint leaves and drizzling over a little extra virgin olive oil.

arancini

Makes **20**
Preparation time **15 minutes**,
  plus making and chilling
  the risotto
Cooking time **1 hour**

2 tablespoons **olive oil**
1 small **carrot**, finely chopped
½ **celery stick**, finely chopped
1 **shallot**, finely chopped
5 oz **ground beef**
8 oz can **chopped tomatoes**
1 tablespoon **tomato paste**
1 quantity **Saffron Risotto**
  (see page 118), chilled
  overnight
¾ cup **all-purpose flour**
2 **eggs**, beaten
4 cups **fresh white bread
  crumbs**
sunflower oil, for deep-frying

Heat the olive oil in a saucepan over a low heat. Add the carrot, celery, and shallot and cook for 8–10 minutes until soft and translucent. Add the ground beef and cook, stirring and breaking up with a wooden spoon, for 5 minutes until lightly golden. Stir in the tomatoes and tomato paste. Bring to a boil, then reduce the heat and simmer very gently for about 30 minutes until the sauce becomes very thick. Allow to cool, then cover and chill for at least 1 hour.

Wet your hands, take 1 tablespoon of the cooked risotto and flatten slightly. Mold around 1 teaspoon of the meat filling to form a ball, making sure that the filling is completely encased. Repeat with the remaining risotto and filling.

Roll each arancino in the flour, then dip in the beaten egg and roll in the bread crumbs to coat.

Heat enough sunflower oil for deep-frying in a deep saucepan to 350–375°F, or until a cube of bread browns in 30 seconds. Add the arancini to the hot oil, in batches, and cook for about 3–4 minutes until golden all over. Remove with a slotted spoon and drain on paper towels. Serve immediately.

For tomato & mozzarella arancini, follow the recipe for Saffron Risotto on page 118, but omit the saffron and replace with 6 tablespoons bought or homemade tomato sauce. Cut 4 oz mozzarella cheese (drained weight) into bite-size pieces. Mold the cooked, chilled risotto around the cheese pieces, then coat in bread crumbs and deep-fry as above.

baked ricotta with bay leaves

Serves **6**
Preparation time **20 minutes**,
   plus soaking and chilling
Cooking time **20 minutes**

4 **sundried tomatoes**
   (dried variety)
2 cups **ricotta cheese**
3 **large eggs**
12 **oven-dried** or **Greek-style**
   black olives, pitted and
   roughly chopped
2 tablespoons **salted capers**,
   rinsed and chopped
butter, for greasing
18 fresh young **bay leaves**
salt and **pepper**

To serve
olive oil
wild arugula leaves
capers

Soak the sundried tomatoes in a bowl of warm water
for 10 minutes. Drain, pat dry, and finely shred.

Push the ricotta through a sieve into a large bowl.
Beat in the eggs, then lightly stir in the sundried
tomatoes, olives, and capers. Season very well with
salt and pepper.

Generously grease 6 x ½ cup ramekins or ovenproof
molds. Put a bay leaf in the base of each and 2 around
the side. Cover and chill to set the butter and keep the
bay leaves in place.

Spoon in the ricotta mixture and level with a spatula.
Set the ramekins on a baking sheet. Bake in a
preheated oven, 375°F, for 20 minutes until set.
Allow to cool, then chill.

Turn the cheeses out onto individual serving plates and
serve at room temperature with a drizzle of olive oil, a
few arugula leaves, and some extra capers. The bay
leaves should not be eaten.

For baked ricotta with arugula, Parmesan, & lemon,
omit the sundried tomatoes, olives, and capers and
replace with 1 ¼ cups wild arugula, roughly chopped,
3 tablespoons grated Parmesan cheese, and the
grated zest of 1 lemon.

salt cod pâté

Serves **4**
Preparation time **10 minutes**,
  plus soaking
Cooking time **15 minutes**

13 oz **salt cod**
1 **bay leaf**
3 **garlic cloves**, peeled but
  kept whole
pinch of **dried red pepper
  flakes**
milk, for poaching
5 tablespoons **extra virgin
  olive oil**, plus extra for
  drizzling
2 tablespoons roughly
  chopped **flat-leaf parsley**
1 **red chili**, seeded and finely
  chopped
salt (optional)
1 small **ciabatta loaf**, cut into
  8 slices and griddled or
  toasted, to serve

Soak the salt cod in a large bowl of cold water for
48 hours, changing the water 5–6 times a day.

Drain the cod and put in a saucepan with the bay
leaf, garlic, and pepper flakes. Pour in enough milk
to completely submerge the cod. Bring to a boil, then
reduce the heat and simmer for 10 minutes. Remove
the cod with a slotted spoon, reserving the poaching
milk and garlic cloves, and leave until cool enough to
handle. Break into flakes, removing and discarding the
skin and any bones.

Process the cod with 5 tablespoons of the reserved
poaching milk and the garlic cloves in a food processor
until smooth. With the motor running, add the oil in a
very slow, steady stream until incorporated.

Stir in the parsley, chopped fresh chili and, if necessary,
a little salt. Drizzle with oil and serve with the griddled or
toasted bread.

For salt cod in batter, prepare the batter as directed
on page 18. Soak and cook 1 lb salt cod as above,
then drain thoroughly and cut into 2 inch pieces.
Heat enough sunflower oil for deep-frying in a deep
saucepan to 350–375°F, or until a cube of bread
browns in 30 seconds. Pat the salt cod pieces dry
with paper towels, then dip in seasoned all-purpose
flour, followed by the batter. Add to the hot oil, in
batches, and cook for 5–6 minutes until golden.
Drain on paper towels. Serve with lemon wedges.

garlic cloves in olive oil

Makes **12**
Preparation time **5 minutes**
Cooking time **20 minutes**

12 large **garlic cloves**
several **rosemary sprigs**
several **thyme sprigs**
1¼ cups **olive oil**

Peel the garlic cloves and put in a small saucepan with the herb sprigs. Cover with the oil and cook over a low heat for about 20 minutes until the garlic is pale golden and soft. Allow the garlic to cool in the oil.

Transfer to a screw-top jar, pour in enough of the oil to submerge the garlic, and store, covered, in the refrigerator, for up to 3 months. Use in salads, potato dishes, purees, risottos, and pizzas. The flavored oil can also be used.

For garlic in basil & chili oil, follow the recipe as above, omitting the rosemary and thyme and replacing them with 1 whole dried red chili. Drop 5 leaves of basil into the jar before adding the cooled garlic and oil.

mozzarella in carrozza

Serves **4**
Preparation time **10 minutes**
Cooking time **15 minutes**

3 **eggs**, lightly beaten
3 tablespoons **whole milk**
½ cup **all-purpose flour**
7 oz **mozzarella cheese**
   (drained weight), cut into
   ¼ inch thick slices
8 slices of **white bread**
12 **basil leaves**
4 tablespoons **olive oil**
salt and **pepper**

Combine the eggs and milk in a bowl and season lightly with salt and pepper. Put the flour in a separate bowl.

Divide the mozzarella slices between 4 bread slices and top each with 3 basil leaves. Lay a second bread slice on top of each to make 4 sandwiches. Press down firmly on each sandwich with the heel of your hand, then cut off and discard the crusts.

Heat half the oil in a large skillet over a medium heat. Turn 2 of the sandwiches, 1 at a time, briefly in the flour to give a light coating, then dip in the egg mixture, making sure that they are well covered. Add to the pan and cook for 3–4 minutes on each side until golden and crisp. Remove and keep warm in a low oven while you cook the second batch of sandwiches in the remaining oil. Serve with a few lettuce leaves, if desired.

For spiced prosciutto & mozzarella in carrozza, combine the eggs and milk as above, but season with salt and ¼ teaspoon chili powder. Follow the recipe to fill the sandwiches with the mozzarella slices together with 1 slice of prosciutto for each, omitting the basil, then coat and cook as above.

prosciutto-wrapped grissini

Makes **20–25**
Preparation time **15 minutes**
Cooking time **5–8 minutes**

½ quantity **Basic Pizza Dough**
(see page 15)
all-purpose flour, for dusting
slices of **prosciutto**, cut into
strips, to serve

Flavorings
coarse sea salt
sesame seeds
poppy seeds
cracked black pepper

Combine the dough balls and roll the dough out thinly on a well-floured work surface into a rectangle. Following the long side of the rectangle, cut into ¼ inch strips. Lightly roll each strip and taper the ends.

Brush the grissini lightly with water and sprinkle with the flavoring of your choice. Transfer to a baking sheet and bake in a preheated oven, 400°F, for 5–8 minutes until crisp and brown. Allow to cool completely.

Twist strips of prosciutto around the grissini to serve.

For cheesy prosciutto-wrapped asparagus, cut 6 slices prosciutto in half, to give you 12 long strips. Wrap these around 12 asparagus spears and lay them on a baking sheet. Drizzle with 1 tablespoon olive oil and sprinkle 1 tablespoon grated Parmesan over the asparagus. Cook under a preheated broiler on high, for 5–6 minutes, until the asparagus is just tender and the ham crispy.

griddled vegetable platter

Serves **4**
Preparation time **10 minutes**,
  plus marinating
Cooking time **20 minutes**

2 **zucchini**, sliced lengthwise
  into ¼ inch thick slices
1 **eggplant**, sliced lengthwise
  into ¼ inch thick slices
1 **yellow bell pepper**, cored,
  seeded, and cut into **1** inch
  wide slices
1 **red bell pepper**, cored,
  seeded, and cut into **1** inch
  wide slices
6 tablespoons **extra virgin**
  olive oil
2 **garlic cloves**, crushed
large pinch of **dried red**
  pepper flakes
handful of small **mint** and/or
  basil leaves
salt

Toss all the prepared vegetables in 2 tablespoons of the oil until well coated.

Heat a ridged griddle pan over a high heat until smoking hot. Add the zucchini and eggplant in batches and cook for 2–3 minutes on each side. Transfer to a bowl and toss with the remaining oil, the garlic, and pepper flakes. Set aside.

Add the peppers in batches to the reheated griddle pan and cook for 3–4 minutes on each side, then combine with the zucchini and eggplant. Season with salt and toss in the herbs.

Cover and allow to marinate at room temperature for 30 minutes. Serve with slices of country bread.

For griddled zucchini with lemon, mint, & Parmesan, omit the peppers and slice 4 large zucchini lengthwise into ¼ inch slices, toss with oil, and then griddle as above. Transfer to a bowl and toss with the remaining oil, the garlic, and pepper flakes as above, adding a handful of small mint leaves, torn, but not the basil. Allow to marinate as above, then serve with a generous topping of Parmesan cheese shavings and the finely grated zest of ½ lemon.

tuna & cranberry bean salad

Serves **4**
Preparation time **15 minutes**,
  plus marinating
Cooking time **3 minutes**

13 oz can **cranberry beans**,
  drained and rinsed
1 tablespoon **water** (optional)
2 tablespoons **extra virgin
  olive oil**
2 **garlic cloves**, crushed
1 **red chili**, seeded and finely
  chopped
2 **celery sticks**, thinly sliced
½ **red onion**, cut into thin
  wedges
7 oz can **tuna in olive oil**,
  drained and flaked
finely grated **zest** and **juice** of
  1 **lemon**
1¼ cups **wild arugula leaves**
salt and **pepper**

Heat the cranberry beans in a saucepan over a medium heat for 3 minutes, adding the measurement water if starting to stick to the base.

Put the oil, garlic, and chili in a large bowl. Stir in the celery, onion, and hot beans and season with salt and pepper. Cover and allow to marinate at room temperature for at least 30 minutes and up to 4 hours.

Stir in the tuna and lemon zest and juice. Gently toss in the arugula leaves, taste and adjust the seasoning with extra salt, pepper, and lemon juice, if necessary.

For a mixed bean salad, heat the cranberry beans as above with a 13 oz can drained and rinsed cannellini beans. Allow to marinate with the other salad ingredients as above, but also adding 2 tablespoons roughly chopped flat-leaf parsley. After marinating, toss in 1¼ cups lamb's lettuce, season with salt and pepper, and serve.

stuffed peppers

Serves **6**
Preparation time **25 minutes**,
  plus steaming and marinating
Cooking time **15 minutes**

6 red, **orange**, or **yellow bell
  peppers**
12 **artichoke hearts in olive
  oil**, drained
24 **anchovy fillets in olive oil**,
  drained
2 **garlic cloves**, sliced
1 tablespoon chopped
  oregano
extra virgin olive oil, for
  drizzling
2 **hard-cooked eggs**, finely
  chopped
salt and **pepper**

Put the whole peppers in a broiler pan and cook under a preheated high broiler or over a barbecue until the skins begin to char. Turn the peppers and continue to cook until charred all over.

Transfer the peppers to a plastic bag, seal, and allow to steam for 10 minutes. Peel off the skins, then cut the peppers in half lengthwise through the stalks and remove and discard the cores and seeds. Arrange the peppers, cut-side up, in a shallow dish.

Cut the artichokes in half and put 2 halves in each pepper half. Lay 2 anchovy fillets over the artichokes. Season well with salt and pepper. Sprinkle over the garlic and oregano, then drizzle with oil.

Cover and allow to marinate in the refrigerator overnight. Serve at room temperature, sprinkled with the chopped hard-cooked eggs.

For broiled peppers in herb oil, broil and peel the peppers as above. Core and seed then cut the flesh into 1 inch strips. Roughly chop 2 rosemary sprigs and 2 thyme sprigs. Toss them into a bowl with the peppers, also adding 1 sliced garlic clove and 1 whole dried chili. Season with salt and pour in 3 tablespoons extra virgin olive oil. Cover and marinate in the refrigerator overnight.

seafood salad

Serves **4**
Preparation time **20 minutes**,
  plus chilling
Cooking time **10 minutes**

1 lb **mussels**, cleaned
  (see page 14)
10 oz **clams**, cleaned
  (see page 14)
1 **onion**, quartered
1 **bay leaf**
10 oz **small squid**, cleaned
  (see page 14) and cut into
  1 inch rounds
10 oz **raw peeled jumbo
  shrimp**
8 small **shelled scallops**,
  with or without roe
juice of 2 **lemons**
2 **garlic cloves**, finely chopped
4 tablespoons **olive oil**
2 **celery sticks**, thinly sliced
1 **carrot**, cut into small cubes
1 **red bell pepper**, cored,
  seeded, and cut into small
  cubes
3 **scallions**, thinly sliced
salt and **pepper**
crusty bread, to serve

Put the shellfish and 6 tablespoons water in a large saucepan with a tight-fitting lid. Cover and bring to a boil over a high heat. Cook, shaking the pan frequently, for 4–5 minutes, or until the shells have opened. Remove with a slotted spoon, discarding any that remain closed. Remove the flesh from the shells and put in a large bowl.

Return the pan with the cooking liquid to a high heat, add 1¾ cups water, the onion, and bay leaf and bring to a boil. Add the seafood and cook for 2–3 minutes until the shrimp turn pink and the scallops are opaque all the way though. Remove with a slotted spoon and add to the shellfish.

Boil the liquid until reduced to 3 tablespoons. Remove from the heat and stir in the lemon juice, garlic, and oil. Season with salt and pepper, pour over the seafood and shellfish, and toss well.

Allow to cool to room temperature, then toss in the remaining ingredients. Cover and chill for at least 30 minutes and up to 24 hours. Serve the salad with crusty bread.

For seafood rice salad, cook the shellfish, then the seafood as above. Remove from the pan, discard the onion and bay leaf, and stir in a large pinch of saffron threads. Boil rapidly until reduced to 6 tablespoons. Toss in 1½ cups freshly cooked long-grain rice. Remove from the heat and stir well. Add the seafood and remaining ingredients as above, but omit the bell pepper.

crudites & garlic anchovy dip

Serves **4–6**
Preparation time **10 minutes**
Cooking time **15 minutes**

3 tablespoons **milk**
6 **garlic cloves**, peeled but
  kept whole
5 oz **anchovy fillets in olive
  oil**, drained and roughly
  chopped
⅓ cup **butter**
5 tablespoons **extra virgin
  olive oil**

Crudites
8 **baby carrots**, peeled
¾ cup **cauliflower florets**
4 **celery sticks**, cut in half
½ **red cabbage**, cut into
  thin wedges
5 **baby fennel**, cut in half
  lengthwise

Put the milk, garlic, and anchovies in a small saucepan over a low heat and cook gently for 15 minutes, without letting the milk come to a boil, until the anchovies have melted into the pan and the garlic is soft.

Use the back of a fork to mash the garlic against the side of the pan. Add the butter and oil and stir until the butter has melted. Transfer to a small serving bowl.

Arrange the crudites in a large serving dish, leaving space for the bowl of sauce, and serve while the sauce is still warm for dipping.

For garlic & caper mayonnaise, to serve in place of the garlic anchovy dip, put 2 egg yolks and 1 crushed garlic clove in a food processor. With the motor running, add 1 cup olive oil in a very slow, steady stream until incorporated, then stir in 1½ tablespoons roughly chopped, rinsed capers in brine. Season with salt and pepper and serve with the crudites as above.

pasta
& pizza

orecchiette with broccoli

Serves **4**
Preparation time **10 minutes**
Cooking time **15 minutes**

1 lb **broccoli**, roughly chopped
13 oz **dried orecchiette**
5 tablespoons **extra virgin olive oil**
2 **anchovy fillets in olive oil**, drained and roughly chopped
large pinch of **dried red pepper flakes**
2 **garlic cloves**, sliced
4 tablespoons freshly grated **Parmesan cheese**, plus extra to serve

Bring a large saucepan of salted water to a boil and tip in the broccoli and pasta. Cook for about 14 minutes, or according to the pasta package instructions, until the pasta is al dente and the broccoli is cooked and starting to fall apart.

Meanwhile, pour the oil into a large skillet and add the anchovies, pepper flakes, and garlic and heat over a very low heat for 5–6 minutes until the anchovies have melted into the oil.

Drain the pasta, reserving a ladleful of the cooking water, and toss the pasta and broccoli into the pan with the anchovy oil. Toss over a high heat for 30 seconds, then pour in the reserved cooking water and continue stirring over the heat for 30 seconds more. Work the Parmesan into the pasta, then serve with an extra sprinkling of Parmesan.

For penne with creamy cauliflower, follow the recipe as above, but replace the broccoli with 1 lb roughly chopped cauliflower and the orecchiette with 13 oz dried penne. Instead of adding the reserved cooking water to the pan at the end of the recipe, stir in 1 cup sour cream with the Parmesan.

wild mushroom lasagna

Serves **6**
Preparation time **20 minutes**,
  plus cooling
Cooking time **45 minutes**

½ cup **unsalted butter**, plus
  extra for greasing
4 tablespoons **all-purpose
  flour**
4 cups **milk**
large pinch of freshly grated
  nutmeg
3 tablespoons roughly
  chopped **flat-leaf parsley**
5 tablespoons freshly grated
  Parmesan cheese
1 tablespoon **olive oil**
1¼ lb **mixed wild
  mushrooms**, trimmed
  and thickly sliced
1 **garlic clove**, crushed
6 tablespoons **dry white wine**
⅔ cup **dried porcini
  mushrooms**, soaked in
  6 tablespoons hot water
  for 10 minutes
10 oz **fresh lasagna sheets**
truffle oil, for drizzling
salt and **pepper**

Melt half the butter in a saucepan over a low heat. Add the flour and cook, stirring with a wooden spoon, for 1–2 minutes until a pale straw color. Remove from the heat and gradually stir in the milk until smooth. Return to a medium heat and cook, stirring constantly, until thick and velvety. Add the nutmeg and season with salt and pepper, then stir in the parsley and 2 tablespoons of the Parmesan. Remove from the heat and allow to cool to room temperature.

Melt the remaining butter with the oil in a large, heavy skillet. Add the fresh mushrooms and cook over a high heat for 2 minutes. Stir in the garlic and cook for 1 minute. Season with salt and pepper. Pour in the wine and porcini and their soaking water. Cook, stirring, until the liquid has evaporated. Stir into the white sauce.

Grease an ovenproof dish, about 8 x 12 inches. Cover the base with a layer of slightly overlapping lasagna sheets. Top with a quarter of the sauce, then continue layering, finishing with a layer of sauce. Sprinkle with the remaining Parmesan. Bake in a preheated oven, 400°F, for 30 minutes. Drizzle lightly with truffle oil and serve with a green salad, if desired.

For mushroom, blue cheese, & spinach lasagna,
follow the recipe above, but stir 3 oz chopped Gorgonzola cheese and 2 cups baby spinach into the white sauce instead of the parsley in the first step, then omit the dried porcini.

fusilli with tuna, capers, & mint

Serves **4**
Preparation time **10 minutes**
Cooking time **12 minutes**

10 oz canned **tuna in olive oil**
4 tablespoons **extra virgin
olive oil**, plus extra for
drizzling
finely grated **zest** of 1 **lemon**
2 **garlic cloves**, crushed
2 tablespoons **capers in
brine**, drained and rinsed
½ **red chili**, seeded and finely
chopped
2 tablespoons roughly
chopped **mint**
13 oz **dried fusilli**
salt

Put the tuna with its oil in a large serving bowl. Break it up with a fork, then stir in the remaining ingredients, except for the pasta. Season with salt. Cover and allow to infuse while you cook the pasta.

Cook the pasta in a large saucepan of salted boiling water for about 10–12 minutes, or according to the package instructions, until al dente.

Drain the pasta and toss into the sauce. Serve immediately with a bottle of extra virgin olive oil for anyone to drizzle a little extra over their serving.

For penne with broiled vegetables, capers, & mint, replace the tuna with 1 ½ cups mixed bottled broiled vegetables in olive oil, such as sweet peppers, zucchini, and eggplant. Drain the vegetables, reserving the oil from the jars. Roughly chop and put in a bowl with 4 tablespoons of the reserved oil and the remaining ingredients as above. Season with salt. Cover and allow to infuse while you cook 13 oz dried penne, instead of the fusilli, as above. Drain and toss with the sauce.

spaghetti with clams & chili

Serves **4**
Preparation time **10 minutes**
Cooking time **20 minutes**

5 tablespoons **extra virgin olive oil**
2 **garlic cloves**, thinly sliced
¼ teaspoon **dried red pepper flakes**
13 oz **dried spaghetti**
⅔ cup **dry white wine**
2 lb **clams**, cleaned (see page 14)
2 tablespoons roughly chopped **flat-leaf parsley**

Heat the oil in the largest skillet you have or a wok over a low heat. Add the garlic and pepper flakes and allow to infuse for 6–8 minutes. If the garlic begins to brown, remove the pan from the heat and let infuse in the heat of the pan.

Cook the pasta in a large saucepan of salted boiling water for 8–10 minutes, or according to the package instructions, until al dente, then drain.

Meanwhile, increase the heat under the skillet and pour in the wine. Boil for 1 minute, then add the clams and cook, stirring, for 4–5 minutes until the shells have opened. Stir in the drained pasta and the parsley and toss over a high heat for 30 seconds. Serve immediately.

For spaghetti with clams, pancetta, & tomatoes,

heat the oil in a large skillet or wok as above. Add 3 oz cubed pancetta and cook for 3–4 minutes until golden and crisp. Add the garlic and allow to infuse over a low heat for 10 minutes. Cook the pasta as above. Add the wine to the skillet and boil for 1 minute as above, then add the clams with 4 oz halved cherry tomatoes and complete the recipe as above.

arugula & tomato tagliatelle

Serves **4**
Preparation time **10 minutes**
Cooking time **8–12 minutes**

1 lb **dried tagliatelle**
3 tablespoons **olive oil**
2 **garlic cloves**, finely chopped
1 lb **very ripe cherry**
   tomatoes, halved
1 tablespoon **balsamic**
   vinegar
3¾ cups **wild arugula leaves**
salt and **pepper**
Parmesan cheese shavings,
   to serve

Cook the pasta in a large saucepan of salted boiling water for 8–12 minutes, or according to package instructions, until al dente, then drain.

Meanwhile, heat the oil in a skillet, add the garlic, and cook, stirring, for 1 minute until golden. Add the tomatoes and cook for barely 1 minute, or until just heated through and beginning to disintegrate.

Sprinkle the tomatoes with the vinegar and allow to evaporate. Toss in the arugula and carefully stir to mix with the tomatoes. Heat through until the arugula is just wilted. Season well with salt and pepper.

Toss the arugula and tomato mixture with the hot cooked pasta and serve immediately, sprinkled with plenty of Parmesan shavings.

For tomato & pancetta tagliatelle, replace the dried tagliatelle with 1 lb egg tagliatelle. Heat the oil in a skillet with 4 oz cubed pancetta. Fry for 4–5 minutes, over a medium heat, until golden then stir in the garlic and cook for 1 minute. Add the tomatoes and complete the recipe as above, omitting the balsamic vinegar and arugula.

roasted tomato & pancetta pasta

Serves **4**
Preparation time **5 minutes**
Cooking time **about 1 hour**

1 lb **cherry tomatoes**
3 tablespoons **olive oil**
13 oz **dried rigatoni** or **penne**
4 oz **pancetta**, cubed
1 **garlic clove**, thinly sliced
2 **shallots**, thinly sliced
large pinch of **dried red
   pepper flakes**
aged balsamic vinegar,
   for drizzling
salt

Put the whole tomatoes in a large roasting pan and drizzle with 2 tablespoons of the oil. Slow-roast in a preheated oven, 300°F, for 1 hour, or until they look semidried.

Meanwhile, cook the pasta in a large saucepan of salted boiling water for about 10–12 minutes, or according to the package instructions, until al dente.

While the pasta is cooking, heat the remaining oil in a large skillet. Add the pancetta, garlic, shallots, and pepper flakes and cook over a low heat for 10 minutes, or until the shallots are golden and the pancetta nice and crispy.

Toss the roasted tomatoes into the skillet, reserving a few for garnishing. Drain the pasta, reserving a ladleful of the cooking water. Add the pasta to the sauce and toss over a high heat for a few seconds. Add the reserved cooking water and continue tossing for another 30 seconds. Serve immediately, garnished with the reserved roasted tomatoes and a drizzle of aged balsamic vinegar.

For roasted tomato, pancetta, & spinach salad, slow-roast the tomatoes and cook the pancetta with the garlic, shallots, and pepper flakes as above. Toss all these ingredients into 2 cups baby spinach in a salad bowl. Beat together 2 tablespoons extra virgin olive oil, 2 teaspoons aged balsamic vinegar, and salt to taste in a small bowl, add to the salad, and toss to coat. Shave over some Parmesan cheese to serve.

fettuccine & dried porcini sauce

Serves **4**

Preparation time **10 minutes**,
plus soaking

Cooking time **20 minutes**

²/₃ cup **dried porcini
mushrooms**, soaked in
³/₄ cup hot water for
10 minutes

2 tablespoons **olive oil**

2 **garlic cloves**, finely chopped

2 tablespoons roughly
chopped **thyme**

2 cups **chicken** or **vegetable
stock**

³/₄ cup **full-bodied red wine**

13 oz **dried fettuccine**

3 tablespoons **unsalted
butter**, cubed

salt and **pepper**

freshly grated **Parmesan
cheese**, to serve

Drain the porcini, reserving the soaking water, and
squeeze out any excess moisture.

Heat the oil in a heavy skillet over a medium heat. Add
the garlic and thyme and cook, stirring, for 30 seconds.
Increase the heat to high. Add the porcini, season with
salt and pepper, and cook, stirring, for 1 minute. Pour in
the reserved soaking water, stock, and wine. Bring to a
boil, then simmer, uncovered, over a very low heat for
15 minutes. Taste and adjust the seasoning.

Meanwhile, cook the pasta in a large saucepan of
salted boiling water for 8–10 minutes, or according
to the package instructions, until al dente. Drain
thoroughly, reserving a ladleful of the cooking water.

Return the pasta to the pan and place over a low heat.
Stir in the sauce and the butter and combine thoroughly.
Add the reserved cooking water and cook, stirring, for a
few seconds until the pasta is well coated and looks
silky. Serve immediately with grated Parmesan.

For fettuccine with creamy mushroom & tarragon
sauce, heat the oil as above, add 10 oz sliced
chestnut mushrooms and 2 finely chopped garlic
cloves and cook, stirring, for 5 minutes. Add the stock
and 6 tablespoons dry white wine, instead of the red,
and bring to a boil. Reduce the heat and simmer as
above, adding ²/₃ cup sour cream and 2 tablespoons
chopped tarragon for the last 5 minutes of cooking.
Combine with the cooked drained fettuccine, as
above, and serve immediately.

lemon, arugula, & basil linguine

Serves **4**
Preparation time **10 minutes**
Cooking time **about 10**
  minutes

13 oz **dried linguine**
¼ cup **unsalted butter**
finely grated **zest** and **juice**
  of 1 **lemon**
6 **basil leaves**, torn
2½ cups **wild arugula leaves**
½ cup freshly grated
  Parmesan cheese
salt and **pepper**

Cook the pasta in a large saucepan of salted boiling water for 8–10 minutes, or according to package instructions, until al dente.

Drain the pasta, reserving half a ladleful of the cooking water. Return the pasta to the pan and place over a low heat. Add all the remaining ingredients, season generously with pepper, and stir until the butter has melted and the pasta is evenly coated. If it looks slightly dry, add some of the reserved cooking water. Serve immediately.

For tortellini with lemon, pea, & basil sauce, instead of the linguine, cook 1 lb fresh spinach and ricotta tortellini in a large saucepan of salted boiling water according to the package instructions until al dente. Meanwhile, put the butter, lemon zest and juice, basil, arugula, and Parmesan as above in a food processor with 1 cup peas, thawed if frozen. Pulse to a coarse paste. Drain the tortellini and return to the pan. Add the sauce, toss with the tortellini, and serve immediately.

meatballs with spaghetti

Serves **4**
Preparation time **20 minutes**
Cooking time **1 hour 20
  minutes**

2 slices of **stale bread**,
  crusts removed
5 tablespoons **milk**
4 tablespoons **olive oil**
6 **scallions** or 1 small **onion**,
  chopped
1 **garlic clove**, chopped
1 ½ lb **lean ground beef**
2 tablespoons freshly grated
  Parmesan cheese
freshly grated **nutmeg**
1 ¼ cups **dry white wine**
13 oz can **chopped tomatoes**
2 **bay leaves**
salt and **pepper**
freshly cooked spaghetti,
  to serve
basil leaves, to garnish

Put the bread in a large bowl, moisten with the milk, and allow to soak.

Heat half the oil in a skillet over a medium heat. Add the scallions or onion and garlic and cook for 5 minutes until soft and just beginning to brown.

Combine the ground beef with the moistened bread, the cooked onions and garlic, and Parmesan, and season with nutmeg, salt, and pepper. Work together with your hands until the mixture is well mixed and smooth. With clean, wet hands, roll the mixture into 28 even-size balls.

Heat the remaining oil in a large, nonstick skillet. Add the meatballs, in batches, and cook until browned all over. Transfer to a shallow ovenproof dish.

Add the wine and tomatoes to the pan and bring to a boil, scraping up any sediment from the base. Add the bay leaves, season with salt and pepper, and boil rapidly for 5 minutes. Pour over the meatballs, cover with foil, and bake in a preheated oven, 350°F, for 1 hour, or until tender. Serve with spaghetti, garnished with basil leaves.

For pork meatballs in a tomato & red pepper sauce,

replace the ground beef with 1 ½ lb ground pork. Shape and brown as above and place in an ovenproof dish with 1 cup bought roasted sweet peppers, cut into 1 inch pieces. Complete the recipe as above.

spinach potato gnocchi

Serves **4–6**
Preparation time **30 minutes**,
  plus resting
Cooking time **25 minutes**

2 lb **floury potatoes**, such as
  russet or Idaho, unpeeled
¼ **whole nutmeg**, freshly
  grated
1¼–2½ cups **all-purpose
  flour**, plus extra for dusting
1 cup **baby spinach**, finely
  chopped
2 **eggs**
salt and **pepper**

Lemon sage butter
¼ cup **butter**
6 whole **sage leaves**
finely grated **zest** of **1 lemon**

Put the potatoes in a saucepan and cover with water.
Cover the pan and bring to a boil. Reduce the heat and
simmer for about 20 minutes until cooked through—a
potato pierced with a blunt knife should slide off the
blade. Drain and leave until cool enough to handle.

Peel the warm potatoes, then pass through a mouli or
ricer to make a light, smooth mash. Transfer to a large
bowl, add the nutmeg, and season with salt and pepper.
Sift in 1¼ cups flour and add the spinach. Break in the
eggs, then gently but quickly work the mixture through
your fingers until it reaches a lumpy bread crumb
consistency. Tip the mixture onto a work surface and
gently knead to a soft, smooth, and pliable dough, adding
more flour if too wet. Be careful not to overwork, or the
gnocchi will lose their light quality.

Divide the dough into 3 pieces and roll each piece
into a finger-thick length. Using a sharp knife, cut into
1 inch pieces. Transfer to a floured tray and allow to
rest for 10–20 minutes. Meanwhile heat the butter
ingredients in a skillet, until the butter has melted and
allow to infuse.

Bring a large saucepan of salted water to a boil. Add the
gnocchi, return to a boil, and cook for 3–4 minutes, or
until they float to the surface. Remove with a slotted
spoon into a skillet with the melted butter. Toss well and
serve immediately.

For arugula gnocchi, replace the spinach with 1¼ cups
wild arugula, finely chopped. Add the zest of 1 lemon to
the potatoes. Complete as above, replacing the sage
leaves with 2 tablespoons chopped parsley.

spaghetti with charred asparagus

Serves **4**
Preparation time **10 minutes**
Cooking time **15 minutes**

1 lb **thin asparagus spears**, trimmed
3–4 tablespoons **extra virgin olive oil**
juice of 1 **lemon**
12 oz **dried spaghetti**
2 **garlic cloves**, roughly chopped
¼–½ teaspoon **dried red pepper flakes**
½ cup **basil leaves**
¼ cup freshly grated **Parmesan cheese**, plus extra to serve (optional)
salt and **pepper**

Brush the asparagus spears with a little of the oil. Cook in a preheated ridged griddle pan or under a preheated high broiler, turning once, until charred and tender. Toss with a little more of the oil, half the lemon juice, and salt and pepper. Set aside.

Cook the pasta in a large saucepan of salted boiling water for 8–10 minutes, or according to the package instructions, until al dente.

Just before the pasta is cooked, heat the remaining oil in a large skillet or wok over a medium heat. Add the garlic with a little salt and cook, stirring, for 3–4 minutes until softened but not browned. Add the pepper flakes and asparagus and heat through.

Drain the pasta, reserving a ladleful of the cooking water, and add both to the skillet with the basil, remaining lemon juice, the Parmesan, and pepper to taste. Serve immediately, with extra Parmesan, if desired.

For pasta salad with mozzarella & asparagus,
complete the first step of the recipe as above and toss into 13 oz freshly cooked penne. Toss in the remaining ingredients and let marinate while the pasta and asparagus cool to room temperature. Roughly chop 7 oz mozzarella and toss into the pasta, adding extra olive oil, if needed.

onion, gorgonzola, & walnut pizza

Serves **4**
Preparation time **10 minutes**,
  plus making the pizza dough
Cooking time **40–45 minutes**

1 quantity **Basic Pizza Dough**
  (see page 15)
a little dressed **arugula**, to
  garnish (optional)

Topping
3 **red onions**
2 tablespoons **extra virgin
  olive oil**, plus extra to drizzle
2 tablespoons chopped **sage**
1 tablespoon **balsamic
  vinegar**
6 oz **Gorgonzola cheese**,
  crumbled
4 tablespoons **sour cream**
½ cup shelled **walnuts**,
  roughly chopped
pepper

Prepare the topping while the pizza dough is rising. Cut each onion into eight wedges, place them in a shallow roasting dish, and drizzle over the oil. Top with half of the sage and season well with salt and pepper. Roast in a preheated oven, 425°F, for 25–30 minutes until soft and caramelized. Add the vinegar and cook for an additional 5 minutes. Allow to cool.

Increase the oven temperature to 475°F, and place a large baking sheet on the middle shelf. Cream together the Gorgonzola and sour cream.

Roll out one piece of pizza dough on a floured surface to form a thin 9 inch round. Transfer to a well floured board or second baking sheet and top with a quarter each of the onions, the cheese mixture, the remaining sage, and walnuts. Season with pepper and drizzle with a little olive oil.

Slide the pizza onto the heated baking sheet. Bake for 10–12 minutes until the base is crisp and the topping melted. Prepare the second pizza while the first one is cooking and so on with all four.

Serve the pizzas garnished with a little arugula, if desired.

For potato & cheese pizza, peel and thinly slice 3 medium potatoes and roast for 20 minutes with sage and oil, in place of the onions, as above. Use to top the pizza with the creamed cheese and walnuts, as above, adding a sprinkling of grated Parmesan, before baking. Omit the vinegar.

pizza fiorentina

Serves **4**
Preparation time **10 minutes**,
 plus making the pizza dough
Cooking time **35 minutes**

1 tablespoon **olive oil**, plus
 extra for drizzling and glazing
2 **garlic cloves**, crushed
1 lb **baby spinach**
1 quantity **Basic Pizza Dough**
 (see page 15)
all-purpose flour, for dusting
¾ cup **passata**
7 oz **mozzarella cheese**
 (drained weight), chopped
20 **black olives**
4 **eggs**
salt and **pepper**

Heat the oil in a large skillet with the garlic for
15 seconds, then add the spinach and cook over a
high heat for 1–2 minutes until just wilted. Season
lightly with salt and pepper.

Heat a baking sheet in a preheated oven, 475°F. Place
1 pizza dough ball on the base only of a well-floured,
9 inch removable-bottomed tart pan. Push down on
the dough with your fingertips, pressing it out to fill
the base, leaving the border slightly thicker. If you get
any tears, forcefully pinch the dough around the hole
back together.

Spoon 3 tablespoons of the passata over the base
and sprinkle with a quarter of the mozzarella, spinach,
and olives. Crack 1 egg onto the pizza, drizzle with oil,
and season lightly with salt and pepper. Brush the
border with oil to glaze. Remove the baking sheet from
the oven, slide the pan onto it, then quickly return to the
oven. Bake for 7–8 minutes until crisp and risen. Serve
immediately. As the first pizza cooks, prepare the next
for the oven.

For spinach, anchovy, & caper pizza, cook the
spinach and prepare the pizza base as above. Brush
with olive oil, then top with a quarter of the mozzarella
and spinach, as above, omitting the olives and egg.
Arrange 5 drained anchovy fillets in olive oil over the
pizza and sprinkle with 1 teaspoon rinsed capers in
brine. Drizzle with chili oil and cook as above. Repeat
to make 3 more pizzas.

prosciutto & artichoke sfincione

Serves **4**

Preparation time **30 minutes**, plus rising

Cooking time **15–20 minutes**

½ oz **fresh yeast** or
  ½ tablespoon **quick-rising active dry yeast**
pinch of **superfine sugar**
1 cup **warm water**
3 cups **all-purpose flour**, plus extra for dusting
2 tablespoons **olive oil**, plus extra for oiling and drizzling
½ teaspoon **salt**
3 tablespoons **sundried tomato paste**
1 **mozzarella cheese**, weighing about 5 oz (drained weight), thinly sliced
4 ripe **plum tomatoes**, cut into long wedges
8 **artichoke hearts in olive oil**, drained and halved
4 large **garlic cloves**, sliced
6 slices **prosciutto**
3 tablespoons freshly grated **Parmesan cheese**
basil leaves, to garnish

Cream the fresh yeast with the sugar in a bowl, then beat in the water. For dried yeast, dissolve the yeast in a bowl with the sugar, water, and 2 tablespoons of the flour. Cover with a moist cloth and allow to stand in a warm place for 10 minutes until foamy.

Sift the flour into a large bowl and make a well in the center. Add the yeast mixture, oil, and salt to the well and mix with a round-bladed knife, then with your hands, until the dough comes together. Knead on a floured work surface for about 10 minutes until smooth and elastic. It should be quite soft, but if it is too soft to handle, add a little more flour. Put in an oiled bowl, cover with a moist cloth, and allow to rise in a warm place for 1 hour, or until doubled in size.

Knock the dough back and roll out to a 12 inch circle, leaving the border slightly thicker. Slide onto a large floured baking sheet.

Spread the tomato paste over the pizza base. Arrange half the mozzarella on top. Sprinkle with the tomatoes, artichokes, and garlic. Drape the prosciutto over the pizza. Sprinkle with the Parmesan and remaining mozzarella. Drizzle with oil and bake in a preheated oven, 475°F, for 15–20 minutes until golden. Serve garnished with basil leaves.

For tomato, onion, and anchovy sfincione, prepare the dough as above. For the topping, cook 1 large sliced onion in 2 tablespoons olive oil. Add 1¼ cups passata, 1 crushed garlic clove, and 8 chopped anchovy fillets. Sprinkle with 5 oz chopped mozzarella and bake as above.

pizza with speck & dolcelatte

Serves **4**
Preparation time **15 minutes**,
  plus making the pizza dough
Cooking time **35 minutes**

¾ cup **passata**
5 large **basil leaves**, torn,
  plus extra to garnish
1 **garlic clove**, crushed
1 tablespoon **extra virgin
  olive oil**, plus extra for
  glazing
1 quantity **Basic Pizza Dough**
  (see page 15)
all-purpose flour, for dusting
4 oz **mozzarella cheese**
  (drained weight), torn into
  chunks
12 slices of **speck**
3 oz **dolcelatte cheese**,
  broken into pieces
salt

Combine the passata, basil, garlic, and oil in a bowl. Season with salt, cover, and allow to infuse for 15 minutes.

Heat a baking sheet in a preheated oven, 475°F. Place 1 pizza dough ball on the base only of a well-floured, 9 inch removable tart pan. Push down on the dough with your fingertips, pressing it out to fill the base, leaving the border slightly thicker. If you get any tears, forcefully pinch the dough around the hole back together.

Spoon 3 tablespoons of the passata mix over the base and sprinkle with a quarter of the mozzarella. Brush the border with oil to glaze. Remove the heated baking sheet from the oven, slide the pan on to it, then quickly return to the oven. Bake for 7–8 minutes until crisp and risen. Top with 3 slices of speck, then half the dolcelatte. Serve immediately, garnished with a little torn basil. As the first pizza cooks, prepare the next for the oven.

For pizza with smoked mozzarella, prosciutto, & arugula, prepare the passata mixture and pizza base as above. Top the tomato mixture with 4 oz smoked mozzarella slices, divided between the 4 pizza bases. Bake as above, then top each pizza with 3 slices of prosciutto and ⅓ cup wild arugula leaves.

eggplant, basil, & ricotta pizza

Serves **4**
Preparation time **10 minutes**,
  plus making the pizza dough
Cooking time **50 minutes**

⅔ cup **passata**
5 large **basil leaves**, torn
1 **garlic clove**, crushed
2–3 small–medium **eggplants**,
  sliced lengthwise into
  ¼ inch thick slices
1 quantity **Basic Pizza Dough**
  (see page 15)
all-purpose flour, for dusting
½ cup **ricotta cheese**, broken
  into small chunks
3 oz **mozzarella cheese**
  (drained weight), roughly
  chopped
olive oil, for glazing
salt
basil leaves, to garnish

Combine the passata, basil, and garlic in a bowl.
Season lightly with salt, cover, and allow to infuse while
you cook the eggplants.

Heat a ridged griddle pan over a high heat until
smoking hot. Add the eggplants, in batches, and cook
for 2 minutes on each side until charred on the outside
and soft all the way through.

Heat a baking sheet in a preheated oven, 475°F. Place
1 pizza dough ball on the base only of a well-floured,
9 inch removable-bottomed tart pan. Push down on the
dough with your fingertips, pressing it out to fill the base,
leaving the border slightly thicker. If you get any tears,
forcefully pinch the dough around the hole back together.

Spoon 2 tablespoons of the passata mixture over the
base, top with a quarter of the eggplants, then sprinkle
with a quarter each of the cheeses. Brush the border
with oil, to glaze. Remove the heated baking sheet from
the oven, slide the pan onto it, then quickly return to the
oven. Bake for 7–8 minutes until crisp and risen. Serve
immediately, garnished with basil leaves. As the first
pizza cooks, prepare the next for the oven.

For zucchini & smoked mozzarella pizza, replace
the eggplants with 4 zucchini and griddle as above.
Omit the ricotta and mozzarella and replace with 5 oz
sliced smoked mozzarella.

olive, onion, & rosemary focaccia

Serves **6**

Preparation time **2 hours, 20 minutes**

Cooking time **about 20 minutes**

½ oz **fresh yeast** or
 1½ teaspoons **quick-rising active dry yeast**
large pinch **superfine sugar**
1 cup **warm water**
3 cups **Italian "00" flour** or
 all-purpose flour, plus extra
 for dusting
½ teaspoon **salt**
olive oil, for oiling and drizzling
1 **onion**, thinly sliced
⅓ cup **pitted black olives**
3 **rosemary sprigs**,
 leaves only
coarse sea salt, for sprinkling

Dissolve the yeast in a bowl with the sugar, water, and half the flour. Cover with a moist cloth and allow to stand in a warm place for 15 minutes until foamy.

Stir the salt into the remaining flour, then tip into the yeast mixture. Stir with one hand to form a moist dough. Knead on a floured work surface for 10 minutes until smooth and elastic. It should be very soft and slightly sticky. If too sticky to handle, add a little more flour. Put in an oiled bowl, cover with a moist cloth, and allow to rise in a warm place for 1 hour, or until doubled in size.

Gently knead half the onion and olives into the dough. Transfer to a lightly oiled rectangular baking sheet, about 8 x 12 inches, stretching it to fill the tray. Cover with a moist cloth and allow to rise in a warm place for 30 minutes. Make deep dimples on the surface with your finger. Sprinkle with the rosemary and remaining onion and olives and drizzle with oil. Cover again and allow to rise for 15 minutes.

Sprinkle the top of the focaccia with coarse sea salt. Bake in a preheated oven, 400°F, for 20 minutes. The bread is ready when the base sounds hollow when tapped. If not, bake for 5 minutes more. Turn out onto a wire rack and allow to cool. Eat warm or at room temperature on the same day.

For basil & tomato focaccia, follow the recipe up to the end of the second step. Knead 5 tablespoons chopped basil into the dough, then transfer to the baking sheet and allow to rise for 30 minutes. Make dimples in the surface, sprinkle with 15 whole cherry tomatoes, and allow to rise for 15 minutes. Season and bake as above.

cherry tomato & arugula pizza

Serves **4**

Preparation time **15 minutes**,
  plus making the pizza dough

Cooking time **35 minutes**

12 **cherry tomatoes**
2 **garlic cloves**, crushed
large pinch of **dried red
  pepper flakes**
2 tablespoons **olive oil**, plus
  extra for glazing
1 quantity **Basic Pizza Dough**
  (see page 15)
all-purpose flour, for dusting
5 oz **buffalo mozzarella
  cheese**, drained and torn
  into large pieces
1¼ cups **wild arugula leaves**
salt

Put the tomatoes in a large bowl and crush them
between your fingers. Add the garlic and pepper flakes,
then stir in half the oil. Season with salt, cover, and allow
to infuse.

Heat a baking sheet in a preheated oven, 475°F. Place
1 pizza dough ball on the base only of a well-floured,
9 inch removable-bottomed tart pan. Push down on
the dough with your fingertips, pressing it out to fill
the base, leaving the border slightly thicker. If you get
any tears, forcefully pinch the dough around the hole
back together.

Spoon a quarter of the tomato mixture over the base,
then brush the border with oil to glaze. Remove the
heated baking sheet from the oven, slide the pan onto
it, then quickly return to the oven. Bake for 7–8 minutes
until crisp and risen. Sprinkle with a quarter each of the
mozzarella and arugula and serve immediately. As the
first pizza cooks, prepare the next for the oven.

For mozzarella & arugula pizza rolls, roll out the
whole dough quantity into a rectangle, approximately
½ inch thick. Finely chop the mozzarella and arugula
and sprinkle over the dough with the garlic, pepper
flakes, and olive oil. Roll up the dough, like a jelly roll,
and cut into 1 inch pieces. Lay the rolls on an oiled
baking sheet and bake for 12–15 minutes. Omit the
cherry tomatoes.

soups, rice, & polenta

barley, bean, & porcini soup

Serves **4**

Preparation time **10 minutes,**
   plus soaking

Cooking time **1 hour**
   35 minutes

½ cup **dried cranberry beans**
½ cup **dried cannellini beans**
8 cups **vegetable** or **chicken**
   stock
2 **celery sticks**, cubed
1 large **carrot**, cubed
1 **onion**, cubed
1 **bay leaf**
¼ teaspoon **dried red pepper**
   flakes
⅓ cup **pearl barley**
½ cup **dried porcini**
   mushrooms
2 tablespoons roughly
   chopped **flat-leaf parsley**
salt and **pepper**

To serve

freshly grated **Parmesan**
   cheese
extra virgin olive oil

Put the dried beans in a large bowl, cover with cold water, and allow to soak overnight.

Drain the soaked beans, put in a large saucepan, and cover with the stock. Stir in the vegetables, bay leaf, and pepper flakes and bring to a boil. Reduce the heat and skim off any scum that has risen to the surface. Simmer, uncovered, for 1 hour.

Stir the pearl barley and porcini into the pan and quickly return to a boil. Skim off any scum, reduce the heat, and simmer for another 30 minutes, or until the beans and barley are very tender.

Add the parsley, then check the seasoning, adding salt and pepper to taste. Serve with a sprinkling of grated Parmesan and a light drizzle of extra virgin olive oil.

For bean, pasta, & red mullet soup, soak 1 cup dried cranberry beans in cold water overnight, then cook with the stock, vegetables, bay leaves, and pepper flakes, as in the second step above, increasing the cooking time to 1½ hours. Increase the heat to a rapid boil and stir in 5 oz dried small pasta shapes. Cook for 6 minutes, then add 8 oz red mullet fillets, cut into 1½ inch pieces. Cook for an additional 2 minutes, or until the pasta is al dente. Sprinkle with 2 tablespoons roughly chopped flat-leaf parsley and drizzle with extra virgin olive oil to serve.

chestnut, rice, & pancetta soup

Serves **4**
Preparation time **10 minutes**
Cooking time **35 minutes**

¼ cup **butter**
5 oz **pancetta**, cubed
1 **onion**, finely chopped
7 oz package **vacuum-packed cooked chestnuts**
¾ cup **arborio, carnaroli,** or **vialone nano rice**
2 cups **chicken stock**
⅔ cup **milk**
salt and **pepper**

Melt half the butter in a saucepan over a medium heat. Add the pancetta and onion and cook for 10 minutes. Cut the chestnuts in half and add to the pan with the rice and stock. Bring to a boil, then reduce the heat and simmer for 20 minutes, or until most of the liquid has been absorbed and the rice is tender.

Heat the milk in a small saucepan until tepid, then stir into the rice with the remaining butter and season the dish with salt and pepper. Cover and allow to stand for 5 minutes before serving.

For fennel, rice, & pancetta soup with garlic & anchovies, follow the recipe above, but replace the onion with 1 large fennel bulb, thinly sliced, omit the chestnuts, and replace the milk with 5 tablespoons of the Garlic Anchovy Dip on page 50.

94

pumpkin & garlic soup

Serves **6–8**
Preparation time **30 minutes**
Cooking time **45 minutes**

1½ lb **pumpkin**, peeled,
  seeded, and cubed
6 **garlic cloves**, unpeeled
4 tablespoons **olive oil**
2 **onions**, thinly sliced
2 **celery sticks**, chopped
¼ cup **long-grain rice**
6 cups **chicken** or **vegetable
  stock**, plus extra if needed
4 tablespoons chopped **flat-
  leaf parsley**
salt and **pepper**

Put the pumpkin in a large roasting pan with the garlic cloves and toss with 2 tablespoons of the oil. Roast in a preheated oven, 400°F, for about 30 minutes until the pumpkin is very tender and beginning to brown.

Meanwhile, heat the remaining oil in a large saucepan over a low heat. Add the onions and celery and cook for 10 minutes until just beginning to brown. Stir in the rice and stock. Bring to a boil, then reduce the heat, cover, and simmer for 15–20 minutes until the rice is tender.

Allow the pumpkin and garlic to cool slightly, then pop the garlic cloves out of their skins and mash them with a fork. Add to the saucepan with the pumpkin and bring to a boil, then simmer for 10 minutes.

Roughly blend the soup in a food processor or blender and return to the pan. Season with salt and pepper. Add extra stock if too thick. Reheat and stir in the parsley. Serve with Parmesan Chips (see below), if desired.

For Parmesan chips, to serve as an accompaniment, spoon 1¼ cups grated Parmesan cheese in small mounds onto a baking sheet lined with nonstick parchment paper. Flatten with the back of a spoon. Sprinkle some fennel seeds and finely chopped chili on top, if desired. Bake in the same oven as the pumpkin and garlic for 3–6 minutes until golden. Remove and leave for 2 minutes to set, or curl over a rolling pin. Carefully lift off the paper or rolling pin and allow to cool completely. Serve separately or sprinkled over the soup.

seafood & fregola soup

Serves **4**
Preparation time **20 minutes**
Cooking time **20 minutes**

6 cups **fish stock**
8 oz **dried fregola** or other
   dried small pasta shape
4 tablespoons **extra virgin
   olive oil**
10 **cherry tomatoes**, halved
2 **garlic cloves**, sliced
3 **anchovy fillets in olive oil**,
   drained and roughly chopped
¼ teaspoon **dried red pepper
   flakes**
6 tablespoons **dry white wine**
1 lb **mussels**, cleaned
   (see page 14)
12 oz **clams**, cleaned
   (see page 14)
10 oz **squid rings**
12 **raw shelled jumbo
   shrimp**
4 tablespoons roughly
   chopped **flat-leaf parsley**
salt (optional)

Bring the stock to a boil in a saucepan, add the pasta and cook for 14–16 minutes, or according to the package instructions, until al dente.

Meanwhile, heat the oil in a large skillet or wok over a low heat. Add the tomatoes, garlic, anchovies, and pepper flakes and cook for 5 minutes, or until the anchovies have melted into the pan and you can smell the aroma of the garlic.

Pour in the wine, bring to a boil, and boil for 1 minute. Add all the seafood and cook, stirring, for 4–5 minutes until the mussels and clams have opened. Discard any that remain closed.

Tip the seafood mixture into the pan with the pasta. Add the parsley, season with salt, if necessary, and stir well. Serve immediately.

For pancetta, potato, & fregola soup, cook the pasta as above, but replace the fish stock with 6 cups chicken or vegetable stock. Heat 1 tablespoon olive oil in a separate saucepan. Add 1 chopped onion, 2 sliced celery sticks, and 4 oz cubed pancetta and cook over a low heat for 5 minutes. Add 2 cups peeled, cubed potatoes and 6 tablespoons dry white wine. Cook for about 10 minutes until the potatoes are tender, then add this mixture to the pan with the pasta. Serve with a drizzle of extra virgin olive oil.

white bean soup

Serves **6**

Preparation time **35 minutes**

Cooking time **1 hour 10 minutes**

1¼ cups **dried white beans**, such as navy or cannellini, soaked overnight in cold water

chicken or **vegetable stock** (optional)

handful of **sage leaves**

5 tablespoons **olive oil**

2 **garlic cloves**, finely chopped

2 tablespoons chopped **sage** or **rosemary**

salt and **pepper**

To garnish

roughly chopped **flat-leaf parsley**

Toasted Garlic & Chili Oil (optional)

Drain the beans and put in a flameproof casserole with a tight-fitting lid. Cover with stock or water to a depth of 2 inches above the beans and push in the sage leaves. Bring to a boil, then cover and bake in a preheated oven, 325°F, for about 1 hour, or until tender. The beans may not take this long, depending on their freshness, so test after 40 minutes. Leave in their cooking liquid.

Put half the beans, the cooked sage leaves, and all the cooking liquid into a food processor or blender and process until smooth. Pour the puree back into the casserole with the remaining beans. Add extra stock or water if too thick.

Heat the oil in a skillet over a low heat. Add the garlic and cook, stirring, until soft and golden. Add the chopped sage or rosemary and cook, stirring, for 30 seconds. Stir into the soup and reheat until boiling, then simmer gently for 10 minutes. Season well with salt and pepper. Serve immediately, garnished with chopped parsley and drizzled with Toasted Garlic & Chili Oil (see below), if desired.

For toasted garlic & chili oil, to serve as an accompaniment, heat 5 tablespoons olive oil in a skillet. Add 4 thinly sliced garlic cloves and cook over a medium heat until golden (don't let it overbrown or it will become bitter), then stir in a large pinch of dried red pepper flakes. Spoon the garlic and oil over the soup.

tomato & bread soup

Serves **4**

Preparation time **15 minutes**

Cooking time **40 minutes**

2 tablespoons **olive oil**

1 small **onion**, finely chopped

1 **celery stick**, thinly sliced

8 oz **day-old rustic bread**, sliced and crusts removed

3 **garlic cloves**, crushed

2 lb **ripe tomatoes**, roughly chopped

4 cups **vegetable** or **chicken stock**

12 **cherry tomatoes**, halved

15 large **basil leaves**

extra virgin olive oil, for drizzling

salt

Heat the oil in a large, heavy saucepan over a low heat. Add the onion and celery and cook for 10 minutes until softened and translucent.

Meanwhile, lightly toast the bread until dried and just beginning to brown, then break it into chunks.

Add the garlic to the saucepan and cook, stirring, for 1 minute, then tip in the toasted bread and tomatoes and cook for 5 minutes until the bread disintegrates into the tomatoes. Stir in the stock and simmer gently for 15 minutes. Add the cherry tomatoes and half the basil and simmer for an additional 5 minutes.

Season with salt, cover, and allow to stand for 5 minutes. Drizzle with extra virgin olive oil and sprinkle with the remaining basil to serve.

For roasted tomato, bread, & balsamic soup, put all the ingredients listed above, except for the bread, stock, and extra virgin olive oil, in a roasting pan with 1 tablespoon balsamic vinegar. Drizzle with olive oil and season with salt and pepper. Roast in a preheated oven, 325°F, for 45 minutes until thickened and caramelized. Bring the stock to a boil in a saucepan, stir in the roasted vegetables, and return to a boil. Divide the toasted bread chunks between 4 soup bowls and spoon over the soup. Serve with an extra drizzle of balsamic vinegar.

fennel soup with olive gremolata

Serves **4**
Preparation time **20 minutes**
Cooking time **40 minutes**

5 tablespoons **extra virgin olive oil**
3 **scallions**, chopped
1½ cups thinly sliced **fennel**, reserve any green fronds for the gremolata and chop them finely
1 **potato**, diced
finely grated zest and juice of 1 **lemon**
3 cups **chicken** or **vegetable stock**
salt and **pepper**

Gremolata
1 small **garlic clove**, finely chopped
finely grated zest of 1 **lemon**
4 tablespoons chopped **parsley**
16 **black olives**, pitted and chopped

Heat the oil in a large saucepan, add the onions, and cook for 5–10 minutes until beginning to soften. Add the fennel, potato, and lemon zest, and cook for 5 minutes until the fennel begins to soften. Pour in the stock and bring to a boil. Turn down the heat, cover the pan and simmer for about 25 minutes or until the ingredients are tender.

Make the gremolata: mix together the garlic, lemon zest, chopped fennel fronds, and parsley then stir the chopped olives into the herb mixture. Cover and chill.

Blend the soup and pass it through a sieve to remove any strings of fennel. The soup should not be too thick, so add more stock if necessary. Return it to the rinsed pan. Taste and season well with salt, pepper, and plenty of lemon juice. Pour into warmed bowls and sprinkle each serving with a portion of the gremolata.

For a fennel & almond soup with orange & olive gremolata, add ½ cup blanched almonds to the pan with the onions. Complete the recipe as above, omitting the potato. Make the gremolata as above, replacing the lemon with the finely grated zest of 1 orange.

ribollita

Serves **4**
Preparation time **15 minutes**
Cooking time **45 minutes**

1 ¼ lb **cavolo nero** (black
  cabbage)
2 tablespoons **extra virgin
  olive oil**, plus extra for
  drizzling
2 **celery sticks**, diced
1 **onion**, thinly sliced
1 large **carrot**, finely chopped
1 ¾ cups finely diced **potatoes**
13 oz can **plum tomatoes**,
  drained
13 oz can **cannellini beans**,
  drained and rinsed
1 **bay leaf**
4 **thyme sprigs**
6 cups **vegetable** or **chicken
  stock**
4 slices of **stale ciabatta
  bread**, torn into bite-size
  pieces
salt and **pepper**

Remove the thick stalks of the cabbage by holding the stems with one hand and using the other hand to strip away the leaves. Discard the stalks and roughly shred the leaves.

Heat the oil in a saucepan over a low heat. Add the celery, onion, and carrot and cook for 8–10 minutes until soft and translucent. Stir in the cabbage, potatoes, tomatoes, half the cannellini beans, the bay leaf, and thyme, then pour in the stock, season with salt and pepper, and bring to a boil. Reduce the heat and simmer, covered, for 30 minutes, until the vegetables are meltingly tender and the stock richly flavored.

Use a potato masher or fork to mash the remaining beans, then add to the soup, stirring well. Add the bread and continue stirring while it soaks up the soup. The ribollita should be thick enough so that it can be eaten with a fork, but if it starts to look dry, add a little water. Serve with a generous drizzle of oil.

For spring ribollita, follow the recipe above, but omit the cabbage. Cut 1 zucchini into cubes and 4 oz green beans into 1 ½ inch pieces, then stir into the pan after the stock has come to a boil, together with ⅔ cup shelled fava beans. Complete the recipe as above.

clam & zucchini soup

Serves **4**
Preparation time **15 minutes**
Cooking time **1 hour**
  20 minutes

1 ½ lb fresh **baby clams**
  or **cockles**, cleaned
  (see page 14)
3 tablespoons **olive oil**
2 large **garlic cloves**, 1 finely
  chopped and 1 bruised
1 ½ lb **zucchini**, thickly sliced
finely grated zest and juice of
  1 **lemon**
1 tablespoon chopped
  marjoram
4 cups **vegetable stock** or
  water
4 thick slices **bread**, toasted
salt and **pepper**
extra olive oil, to serve

Bring ½ inch water to a boil in a saucepan, add the clams, and steam until they open. Reserve the juice and remove half of the clams from their shells, keeping the remaining clams in their shells. Discard any clams that have not opened.

Heat the olive oil in a saucepan, add the chopped garlic, and cook gently until golden but not brown. Add the zucchini, lemon zest, and marjoram and turn them in the oil and garlic. Pour in the stock, season lightly with salt and pepper, and bring to simmering point. Cover the pan and simmer for about 10 minutes or until the zucchini are soft.

Pass the soup through a coarse food mill and return it to the pan. Add the reserved clam juice and the shelled clams. If the soup is too thick, add extra stock or water. Taste and season with salt and pepper and a little lemon juice. Stir in the clams in their shells.

Rub the toasted bread with the bruised garlic clove. Place a slice in each bowl and ladle on the soup. Drizzle each serving with olive oil and serve immediately.

For spiced jumbo shrimp & zucchini soup, replace the clams with 1 lb shelled raw jumbo shrimp. Follow step 2 and pass the soup through a food mill. Heat 2 tablespoons olive oil in a large skillet and use to fry the shrimp with 2 crushed garlic cloves and a large pinch of dried red pepper flakes for 3 minutes, until golden. Add ½ cup dry white wine, boil for 1 minute then season with salt and stir into the soup. Serve with toast and a drizzle of olive oil, as above.

radicchio risotto with pancetta

Serves **4**
Preparation time **10 minutes**
Cooking time **40 minutes**

4 slices of **pancetta**
¼ cup **salted butter**
1 **onion**, finely chopped
2 **garlic cloves**, finely chopped
1 cup **arborio**, **carnaroli,** or
  vialone nano rice
1¾ cups **Barolo** or other full-
  bodied red wine
6 oz **radicchio**, sliced
2½ cups **vegetable** or
  chicken stock, simmering
3 tablespoons freshly grated
  Parmesan cheese, plus
  extra to serve

Cook the pancetta on a baking sheet in a preheated oven, 400°F, for 5–6 minutes, or until golden brown. Set aside.

Melt half the butter in a heavy saucepan over a low heat. Add the onion and cook for 10 minutes until softened. Add the garlic and rice and cook, stirring, for 1 minute. Pour in half the wine and cook, stirring, until absorbed. Add the remaining wine and cook, stirring, until absorbed.

Stir in the radicchio and 3 ladlefuls of the simmering stock. Slowly simmer, stirring constantly, until the stock has been absorbed and the rice parts when a wooden spoon is run through it. Add another ladleful of stock and continue to cook, stirring and adding the stock in ladlefuls, for 18–20 minutes until the rice is creamy and almost tender to the bite.

Remove from the heat and add the remaining butter and the Parmesan. Stir vigorously for 15 seconds. Cover with a tight-fitting lid and let stand for 1 minute. Serve immediately topped with the pancetta, with extra Parmesan on the side.

For watercress & lemon risotto, follow the recipe above from the second step, replacing the red wine with ¾ cup dry white wine, omitting the radicchio, and using 3¾ cups simmering vegetable stock. Once the risotto is cooked, stir in 2½ cups roughly chopped watercress and the finely grated zest of 1 lemon with the butter and Parmesan. Let stand, as above, before serving.

tomatoes stuffed with rice

Serves **4**
Preparation time **15 minutes**,
   plus standing
Cooking time **35 minutes**

4 large or 8 small **tomatoes**,
   about 1 ¼ lb in total
2 **garlic cloves**, crushed
scant ½ cup **arborio,
   carnaroli,** or **vialone
   nano rice**
6 **basil leaves**, torn
2 tablespoons **extra virgin
   olive oil**, plus extra for oiling
   and drizzling
salt and **pepper**

Cut a slice off the stalk end of each tomato and set
aside to use as lids. Scoop the pulp out of the tomatoes
and chop. Transfer to a large bowl, taking care not to
lose any of the tomato juices, and add the garlic, rice,
and basil. Season with salt and pepper and stir in
1 tablespoon of the oil. Cover and allow to stand at
room temperature for 1 hour, for the rice to soak up
all the juices.

Stuff the tomatoes with the rice mixture, then transfer
to an oiled baking dish. Top with their reserved lids
and drizzle with the remaining oil. Bake in a preheated
oven, 350°F, for 35 minutes until the tomatoes are
soft and the rice is cooked through. Serve warm or
at room temperature.

**For tomatoes stuffed with rice, capers, anchovies,
& olives**, prepare the tomatoes as above. For the filling,
add 1 tablespoon each chopped flat-leaf parsley, pitted
black olives, and rinsed capers in brine to the chopped
tomato pulp with the garlic and rice. Toss in 2 drained,
chopped anchovy fillets in olive oil and season with
pepper only. Complete the recipe as above.

pumpkin, sage, & chili risotto

Serves **6**
Preparation time **20 minutes**
Cooking time **40 minutes**

½ cup **butter**
1 large **onion**, finely chopped
1 **fresh** or **dried red chili**,
   seeded and finely chopped
1 lb **pumpkin**, peeled, seeded,
   and roughly chopped
2½ cups **arborio**, **carnaroli**, or
   vialone nano rice
6 cups **chicken** or **vegetable
   stock**, simmering
3 tablespoons chopped **sage**,
   plus extra sprigs to garnish
¾ cup freshly grated
   Parmesan cheese
salt and **pepper**

Melt half the butter in a large saucepan over a low heat. Add the onion and cook for 10 minutes until softened. Add the chili and cook, stirring, for 1 minute. Add the pumpkin and cook, stirring constantly, for 5 minutes.

Add the rice and cook, stirring, for 2 minutes. Add a large ladleful of the simmering stock. Slowly simmer, stirring constantly, until the stock has been absorbed and the rice parts when a wooden spoon is run through it. Add another ladleful of stock and continue to cook, stirring and adding the stock in ladlefuls, for about 20 minutes until the rice is creamy and almost tender to the bite and the pumpkin is beginning to disintegrate. Season well with salt and pepper.

Remove from the heat and add the chopped sage, remaining butter, and the Parmesan. Stir vigorously for 15 seconds. Cover with a tight-fitting lid and allow to stand for a few minutes. Serve garnished with sage sprigs.

For pumpkin risotto with amaretto cookies & almonds, cook the risotto as above, omitting the sage and replacing the Parmesan with 2 crushed amaretto cookies. Serve with a sprinkling of toasted flaked almonds.

asparagus, pea, & mint risotto

Serves **4**
Preparation time **10 minutes**
Cooking time **45 minutes**

1 lb **asparagus spears**
4 cups **vegetable** or **fish stock**
¼ cup **butter**
1 **onion**, finely chopped
1½ cups **arborio**, **carnaroli**, or **vialone nano rice**
⅔ cup **dry white wine**
⅔ cup shelled **fresh** or **frozen peas**
4 tablespoons freshly grated **Parmesan cheese**, plus extra to serve
handful of **mint leaves**, roughly chopped

Cut the asparagus in half, at an angle, separating the tips from the thicker stalks. Reserve the tips. Put the stalks in a saucepan with the stock and bring to a boil. Boil for 5 minutes, then reduce the heat to a simmer. Remove the asparagus with a slotted spoon and process in a food processor or blender until pureed.

Melt half the butter in a heavy saucepan over a low heat. Add the onion and cook for 10 minutes until softened. Add the rice and cook, stirring, for 1 minute. Add the wine and cook, stirring, until absorbed. Stir in the pureed asparagus.

Add 2 ladlefuls of the simmering stock. Slowly simmer, stirring constantly, until the stock has been absorbed and the rice parts when a wooden spoon is run through it. Add another ladleful of stock and continue to cook, stirring and adding the stock in ladlefuls, reserving 2 ladlefuls, for 16–18 minutes until the rice is creamy and almost tender to the bite.

Add the peas and the reserved asparagus tips and stock and continue cooking until the stock is almost absorbed. Remove from the heat and stir in the Parmesan, mint, and remaining butter. Stir vigorously for 15 seconds. Cover with a tight-fitting lid and allow to stand for 2 minutes. Serve immediately with extra Parmesan on the side.

For asparagus & pancetta risotto, follow the recipe above, but cook 5 oz cubed pancetta with the onion. Omit the peas and replace the mint with 2 tablespoons roughly chopped flat-leaf parsley.

saffron risotto

Serves **4**
Preparation time **5 minutes**
Cooking time **35 minutes**

¼ cup **butter**
1 **onion**, finely chopped
1½ cups **arborio**, **carnaroli**,
   or **vialone nano rice**
⅔ cup **dry white wine**
4 cups **beef** or **vegetable**
   stock, simmering
½ teaspoon **saffron threads**
4 tablespoons freshly grated
   Parmesan cheese, plus
   extra to serve

Melt half the butter in a heavy saucepan over a low heat. Add the onion and cook for 10 minutes until softened. Add the rice and cook, stirring, for 1 minute. Pour in the wine and cook, stirring, until absorbed.

Add 2 ladlefuls of the simmering stock and the saffron. Slowly simmer, stirring constantly, until the stock has been absorbed and the rice parts when a wooden spoon is run through it. Add another ladleful of stock and continue to cook, stirring and adding the stock in ladlefuls, for 18–20 minutes until the rice is creamy and almost tender to the bite.

Remove from the heat and stir in the Parmesan and remaining butter. Stir vigorously for 15 seconds. Cover with a tight-fitting lid and allow to stand for 1 minute. Serve immediately with extra Parmesan on the side.

For shrimp, zucchini, & saffron risotto, follow the recipe above, but when the rice has been cooking for 15 minutes and most of the stock has been incorporated, stir 1 roughly grated zucchini and 16 raw peeled jumbo shrimp into the rice mixture. Continue adding the remaining stock and complete the recipe as above, but omit the Parmesan.

baked polenta with gorgonzola

Serves **4**
Preparation time **5 minutes**
Cooking time **15 minutes**

3 cups **water**
¼ cup **instant polenta**
¼ cup **butter**, plus extra for
  greasing
7 oz **Gorgonzola cheese**,
  broken into pieces
5 tablespoons freshly grated
  Parmesan cheese
10 **cherry tomatoes**
salt and **pepper**

Bring the measurement water to a boil in a large, heavy saucepan. Set aside 2 tablespoons of the polenta to use for the topping and put the remaining polenta in a pitcher. Pour into the water in a slow but steady stream, stirring vigorously with a wooden spoon to prevent any lumps forming. Reduce the heat to a slow simmer and cook, stirring frequently, for about 5 minutes, or until the polenta is thick and comes away from the side of the pan. Stir in the butter and season with salt and pepper.

Pour half the polenta into a greased baking dish, about 10 x 7 inches. Top with the Gorgonzola and half the Parmesan. Cover with the remaining cooked polenta, then top with the tomatoes. Stir the remaining Parmesan into the reserved uncooked polenta for the topping and sprinkle over the dish.

Cook under a preheated medium broiler for 4–5 minutes until the tomatoes are slightly softened and beginning to char. Serve steaming hot.

For griddled herbed polenta, cook the polenta as in the first step, then stir in 2 tablespoons each roughly chopped flat-leaf parsley, basil, and wild arugula leaves and add 4 tablespoons grated Parmesan cheese. Tip into a 2 lb loaf pan and allow to cool at room temperature. Turn the polenta out and cut into ½ inch slices. Brush with olive oil, then cook on a preheated ridged griddle pan over a high heat for 1 minute on each side.

polenta fries

Serves **4**

Preparation time **15 minutes**, plus chilling

Cooking time **35 minutes**

¼ cup **butter**

2½ cups **water**

1 teaspoon **salt**

¾ cup **instant polenta**

sunflower oil, for oiling and deep-frying

all-purpose flour, for coating

paprika, for sprinkling

salt

Put the butter, measurement water, and salt in a heavy saucepan and bring to a boil. Put the polenta in a pitcher and pour into the water mixture in a slow but steady stream, stirring vigorously with a wooden spoon to prevent lumps forming. Reduce the heat to a slow simmer and cook, stirring frequently, for about 5 minutes, or until the polenta is thick and comes away from the side of the pan.

Transfer the polenta to a shallow oiled dish, smooth the top, and allow to cool. Cover and chill until firm.

Turn the polenta out on to wet waxed paper and cut into thick fries with a wet knife.

Heat enough oil for deep-frying in a deep saucepan to 350–375°F, or until a cube of bread browns in 30 seconds. Roll the fries in a little flour to coat, add to the hot oil, in batches, and cook for 6–8 minutes until pale golden brown and crisp. Remove with a slotted spoon and drain on paper towels. Sprinkle with salt and paprika. Keep warm in a low oven with the door ajar until ready to serve.

For tomato & basil dip, to serve as an accompaniment, blend 4 ripe tomatoes with 1 garlic clove, 4 basil leaves, and ½ seeded red chili. Stir in 2 tablespoons extra virgin olive oil and season with salt. Serve with the fries, omitting the paprika.

cheesy polenta & mushrooms

Serves **4**
Preparation time **10 minutes**
Cooking time **15 minutes**

13 oz **mixed wild
mushrooms**, such as
porcini, girolles, and
chanterelles
2 tablespoons **butter**
2 **garlic cloves**, chopped
5 whole **sage leaves**
3 tablespoons **dry vermouth**
salt and **pepper**

Polenta
3 cups **water**
1¼ cups **instant polenta**
½ cup freshly grated
Parmesan cheese
¼ cup **butter**, cubed

Brush away any soil and grit from the mushrooms with a moist cloth, then slice the porcini and tear any other large mushrooms in half. Set aside.

Melt the butter in a large skillet over a medium-high heat. Add the garlic, sage, and the dense, tougher mushrooms and cook for 2–3 minutes. Add the remaining mushrooms, season with salt and pepper, and cook for 2–3 minutes until soft and cooked through. Pour in the vermouth and cook, stirring, for 1 minute.

For the polenta, bring the measurement water to a boil in a large, heavy saucepan. Put the polenta in a pitcher and pour into the water in a slow but steady stream, stirring vigorously with a wooden spoon to prevent any lumps forming. Reduce the heat to a slow simmer and cook, stirring frequently, for about 5 minutes, or until the polenta is thick and comes away from the side of the pan. Stir in the butter and season with salt and pepper.

Divide the polenta between 4 serving plates, then top with the mushrooms.

For cheesy polenta with mushrooms & tomato, cook the mushrooms as above, but replace the rosemary with 3 chopped thyme sprigs and use ⅔ cup full-bodied red wine instead of the vermouth. When the wine has boiled for 1 minute, stir in 1¼ cups passata. Season with salt and pepper and bring to a boil, then simmer for 5 minutes. Cook the polenta as above, then gradually stir in the cheese. Serve with the mushroom and tomato mixture.

fish & seafood

sea bass in a salt crust

Serves **4**
Preparation time **15 minutes**
Cooking time **30 minutes**

1 **sea bass**, about 1 lb, gutted
  and scaled
2 lb **coarse sea salt**
1 **egg white**
1 tablespoon **cold water**

To serve
lemon wedges
extra virgin olive oil

Wash the inside and outside of the sea bass under cold running water and pat dry with paper towels.

Put the sea salt in a bowl. Beat the egg white and measurement water together in a small bowl, then stir into the sea salt.

Spread a layer of the sea salt mixture out in the base of a roasting pan large enough to hold the fish comfortably. Lay the fish on top, then cover the fish with the remaining salt mixture. Pat down, making sure that the fish is completely encased by the salt.

Roast in a preheated oven, 400°F, for 30 minutes. Remove from the oven. Break the salt crust with the back of a large knife and lift off. If there are still a lot of salt crystals on the surface of the fish, brush these off with a pastry brush. Use a spatula to lift the fish onto a serving dish. Serve with lemon wedges and extra virgin olive oil for drizzling, accompanied by steamed vegetables.

For fennel, lemon, & thyme sea bass in a salt crust, pound 2 teaspoons fennel seeds, the finely grated zest of 1 lemon, the leaves of 3 thyme sprigs, and 1 tablespoon olive oil in a mortar with a pestle. Rub the mixture all over the inside and outside of the sea bass. Cover and allow to marinate in the refrigerator for 30 minutes. Prepare the salt mixture and roast the fish in the salt crust as above.

red mullet with salsa verde

Serves **4**
Preparation time **20 minutes**
Cooking time **10 minutes**

4 **red mullet,** gutted and
  scaled
2 tablespoons **olive oil**
1 **lemon**, halved lengthwise
  and thinly sliced
salt and **pepper**

Salsa verde
2 **garlic cloves**, finely chopped
3 **anchovy fillets in olive oil**,
  finely chopped
1 tablespoon **capers in brine**,
  rinsed and finely chopped
4 tablespoons roughly
  chopped **flat-leaf parsley**
2 tablespoons roughly
  chopped **mint**
2 tablespoons roughly
  chopped **basil**
1 tablespoon **red wine
  vinegar**
4 tablespoons **extra virgin
  olive oil**

Combine all the ingredients for the salsa verde in a
bowl and season with salt and pepper. Set aside.

Wash the inside and outside of the fish under cold
running water and pat dry with paper towels. Cut
2–3 deep slashes along the width of both sides of the
fish, then brush all over with the oil. Season with salt
and pepper. Insert a lemon slice into each slash, then
tuck a couple of slices inside each fish.

Lay the fish on a nonstick baking sheet and cook under
a preheated very high broiler, about 4 inches from the
heat source, for about 5 minutes on each side until
cooked through and lightly charred. Serve immediately
with the salsa verde.

For smoked mackerel with potato & salsa verde
salad, boil or steam 1 lb baby new potatoes until tender,
then lightly crush with the back of a spoon. Prepare the
salsa verde as above, but using 5 tablespoons extra
virgin olive oil. Toss the warm potatoes with the dressing.
Replace the red mullet with 4 smoked mackerel fillets.
Break into large flakes and gently toss into the salad.

roast garlic-studded angler fish

Serves **4**

Preparation time **20 minutes,**
  plus marinating

Cooking time **30 minutes**

2 lb **angler fish tail**, trimmed
  and boned (see page 138)

3–4 **bay leaves**

1 teaspoon **fennel seeds**

4 **garlic cloves**, cut into thick
  slivers

4 tablespoons **olive oil**

a few **thyme sprigs**

2 **red bell peppers**, cored,
  seeded, and roughly
  chopped

1 **eggplant**, cut into bite-size
  chunks

2 **zucchini**, cut into bite-size
  chunks

3 **ripe plum tomatoes**, cut
  into chunks

3 tablespoons **lemon juice**

salt and **pepper**

To garnish

2 tablespoons **salted capers**,
  rinsed and chopped

3 tablespoons chopped **flat-
  leaf parsley**

Lay the bay leaves over one fish fillet and sprinkle with the fennel seeds. Lay the other fillet on top and tie at 1 inch intervals with fine string. With the tip of a sharp knife, make slits all over the fish and push in the garlic slivers. Put the oil, thyme, and a little pepper into a glass dish, add the fish, and turn well to coat. Cover and let marinate in the refrigerator for at least 2 hours or overnight.

Remove from the marinade. Pour 2 tablespoons of the marinade into a heavy, nonstick skillet and heat until almost smoking. Add the fish and cook, turning, for 2–3 minutes until sealed. Set aside.

Heat the remaining marinade in the pan. Add the vegetables and quickly brown. Transfer to a heavy, shallow baking dish, set the fish on top and add the tomatoes and lemon juice. Bake in a preheated oven, 425°F, for 20 minutes, basting and turning the vegetables occasionally.

Remove the string and cut the fish into thick slices. Season the vegetables with salt and pepper. Serve the angler fish on the vegetables, garnished with the capers and parsley.

For roasted angler fish with olive paste, omit the marinade. Make a quick olive paste by blending ½ cup pitted black olives, the leaves from 2 sprigs thyme, 1 garlic clove, and 3 tablespoons olive oil. Spread over one angler fish fillet then lay the other fillet on top and tie as above. Seal the fish in a pan with 2 tablespoons olive oil then roast it with the vegetables, as above.

sole with tomatoes & capers

Serves **2**
Preparation time **10 minutes**
Cooking time **25 minutes**

4 tablespoons **olive oil**
1 **garlic clove**, roughly
  chopped
2 **sole**, about 13 oz each,
  skinned (ask your fish
  merchant to do this for you)
¼ cup **all-purpose flour**,
  seasoned with **salt**
6 tablespoons **dry white wine**
¾ cup **passata**
pinch of **superfine sugar**
½ teaspoon **dried oregano**
2 tablespoons **capers in
  brine**, rinsed
salt and **pepper** (optional)

Heat the oil in a large skillet over a low heat. Add the garlic and cook for 10 minutes. Discard the garlic and increase the heat to high.

Pat the sole dry with paper towels, then turn in the seasoned flour to coat both sides. Gently lower into the hot oil and cook for 4–5 minutes on each side until golden (if your pan isn't large enough, cook individually and keep the cooked sole warm in a low oven while you cook the remaining fish). Remove to a warmed serving plate.

Pour the wine into the skillet and cook, stirring well with a wooden spoon to loosen any sediment from the base of the pan, for 1 minute. Add the passata, sugar, oregano, and capers and bring to a boil. Check the seasoning and add salt and pepper if necessary, then spoon the sauce over the fish. Serve immediately.

For sole with lemon, parsley, & garlic, cook the sole as above and keep warm. Melt ¼ cup butter in the skillet over a medium heat and stir in the grated zest of 1 lemon and 2 crushed garlic cloves. Cook for 2 minutes, then remove from the heat and stir in the juice of 1 lemon and 2 tablespoons finely chopped flat-leaf parsley. Spoon over the fish and serve immediately.

sardines stuffed with fennel

Serves **4**
Preparation time **15 minutes**,
    plus cooling
Cooking time **25 minutes**

4 tablespoons **extra virgin
    olive oil**
1 **fennel bulb**, thinly sliced
1 **onion**, thinly sliced
pared **rind** of 1 small **orange**
pared **rind** of 1 **lemon**
1 tablespoon roughly
    chopped **dill weed**
1 teaspoon **fennel seeds**
¼ teaspoon **dried red pepper
    flakes**
2 **garlic cloves**, finely chopped
5 tablespoons **fresh white
    bread crumbs**
2 tablespoons roughly
    chopped **flat-leaf parsley**
4 large or 8 small **sardines**,
    filleted
juice of ½ **lemon**
salt
lemon wedges, to serve

Pour half the oil into a large, heavy skillet and stir in the
fennel and onion. Add the citrus rind, dill, fennel seeds,
and pepper flakes and place the pan over a very low
heat. Cook, stirring frequently, for 12–15 minutes until
the fennel and onion are golden and caramelized, being
careful not to burn. Add the garlic and cook, stirring, for
2 minutes. Remove from the heat and stir in half the
bread crumbs and parsley. Season with salt and allow
to cool.

Drizzle 1 tablespoon of the remaining oil over a large
baking sheet. Add half the sardine fillets, skin-side down.
Season lightly with salt, then spread the fennel mixture
over each fillet. Press a second fillet on top, skin-side
up, and sprinkle with the remaining bread crumbs and
parsley. Drizzle with the remaining oil and squeeze the
lemon juice over the fish. Season again with salt.

Cook under a preheated high broiler for 6–8 minutes
until the fish is opaque all the way through. Serve
with lemon wedges, accompanied by a tomato and
lettuce salad.

For spaghetti with sardine & fennel sauce, cook
13 oz dried spaghetti in a large saucepan of salted
boiling water for 8–10 minutes, or according to the
package instructions, until al dente. Meanwhile, follow
the first step above, omitting the bread crumbs and
adding 8 oz roughly chopped sardine fillets to the
pan with the garlic. Cook for 2 minutes until cooked
through. Drain the pasta, return to the pan, and stir
through the sauce.

angler fish in salsa d'agrumi

Serves **4**
Preparation time **20 minutes**
Cooking time **15 minutes**

1¾ lb **angler fish tail**
all-purpose flour, seasoned
  with **salt** and **pepper**, for
  coating
2 tablespoons **olive oil**
finely grated **zest** and **juice**
  of 1 **lemon**
finely grated **zest** and **juice**
  of 1 **orange**
⅔ cup **dry white wine**
2 tablespoons chopped **flat-
  leaf parsley**
salt and **pepper**

To garnish
pared **orange rind**
parsley sprigs
orange and **lemon wedges**

Trim any membrane and dark meat from the fish.
Remove the central bone by slitting the fish down the
center until you reach the bone. Turn the fish over and
do the same on the other side. Ease out the bone,
gently scraping the flesh away with the tip of a knife.
Cut the fish into large chunks, then toss in seasoned
flour to coat all over, shaking off the excess.

Heat the oil in a nonstick skillet over a medium-high
heat. Add the fish and cook until golden all over.
Remove to a plate.

Add the grated citrus zest and juice to the pan with the
wine and boil rapidly. Reduce the heat, return the fish to
the pan, and simmer gently for 3–4 minutes, or until the
fish is cooked through. Stir in the parsley and salt and
pepper to taste.

Lift the fish out onto a warmed serving dish. Boil the
sauce to reduce it a little more, then pour over the fish.
Serve immediately, garnished with orange rind, parsley
sprigs, and orange and lemon wedges.

For sole in lemon & basil sauce, dust 2 x 13 oz
skinned sole in seasoned all-purpose flour and fry in
the oil, instead of the angler fish, for 2 minutes on each
side, until golden. Remove to a plate then continue the
recipe as above, omitting the orange juice and zest
and adding 5 torn basil leaves to the sauce instead of
the parsley.

swordfish with onion & pine nuts

Serves **4**
Preparation time **10 minutes**
Cooking time **20 minutes**

4 tablespoons **olive oil**
1 **onion**, thinly sliced
1 **celery stick**, sliced
2 tablespoons **golden raisins**
1 **bay leaf**
3 tablespoons **pine nuts**
2 **garlic cloves**, sliced
4 **swordfish steaks**, about
    1 inch thick
all-purpose flour, seasoned
    with **salt** and **pepper**, for
    coating
⅔ cup **dry white wine**

Heat half the oil in a large, heavy skillet over a low heat. Add the onion, celery, golden raisins, and bay leaf and cook for 8–10 minutes until soft and golden. Stir in the pine nuts and garlic and cook for an additional 2 minutes. Remove to a dish.

Heat the remaining oil in the pan over a high heat. Turn the swordfish steaks in the seasoned flour to coat on both sides. Add to the hot oil and cook for 3 minutes on each side until golden brown.

Return the onion mixture to the pan and pour in the wine. Boil vigorously for 2 minutes. Serve immediately.

For tuna with onion & olives, follow the first step above, but omit the golden raisins and replace the pine nuts with ⅓ cup halved, pitted black olives. Continue with the recipe as above, but use 4 tuna steaks, about 1 inch thick, instead of the swordfish steaks.

barbecued shrimp skewers

Serves **4**

Preparation time **10 minutes**,
  plus marinating

Cooking time **5 minutes**

1 **garlic clove**, sliced

3 tablespoons **extra virgin
  olive oil**

1 tablespoon chopped **flat-
  leaf parsley**

finely grated **zest** of 1 **lemon**

20 raw **jumbo shrimp**

salt

lemon wedges, to serve

Put the garlic, oil, parsley, and lemon zest in a
nonreactive bowl and toss in the shrimp. Cover and
allow to marinate in the refrigerator for at least
15 minutes and up to 1 hour.

Heat a ridged griddle pan over a high heat until
smoking hot, or preheat a gas barbecue to high or, if
using a charcoal barbecue, get the coals to the stage
where there are no more flames and the coals are
covered with a thin layer of gray ash.

Thread the shrimp onto metal skewers and season
with salt. Cook for 1–2 minutes on each side until the
shrimp have turned pink and are lightly charred. Serve
immediately with lemon wedges.

For tomato, onion, & bread salad, to serve as an
accompaniment, stir ½ thinly sliced red onion, 1 lb
quartered tomatoes, and 5 torn basil leaves into a
bowl with 3 tablespoons extra virgin olive oil and
1 tablespoon red wine vinegar. Season with salt and
pepper and toss in 3 oz stale rustic bread, cut into
walnut-size pieces. Cover and allow to marinate at
room temperature for 30 minutes before serving.

mussels alla marinara

Serves **4**
Preparation time **15 minutes**
Cooking time **10 minutes**

3 tablespoons **olive oil**
4 **garlic cloves**, chopped
⅔ cup **dry white wine**
13 oz can **chopped tomatoes**
1 small **red chili**, seeded and
  finely chopped
2 tablespoons chopped **flat-
  leaf parsley**, plus extra
  whole leaves to garnish
4 lb **mussels**, cleaned
  (see page 14)
salt and **pepper**

Heat the oil in a large saucepan over a low heat. Add the garlic and cook for about 5 minutes until golden. Add the wine, tomatoes, chili, and chopped parsley and bring to a boil. Season well with salt and pepper.

Add the mussels to the pan, cover, and cook over a high heat, shaking the pan frequently, for 4–5 minutes, or until the shells have opened. Stir well and discard any that remain closed.

Sprinkle the whole parsley leaves over the mussels and serve immediately with crusty bread, if desired.

For squid alla marinara, fry the garlic as above, also adding ½ teaspoon fennel seeds to the pan. Continue following the recipe, replacing the mussels with 1 lb squid rings.

stuffed squid in tomato sauce

Serves **4**

Preparation time **15 minutes**, plus cooling

Cooking time **45 minutes**

8 **squid**, about 1 ¼ lb in total, cleaned (see page 14)

4 tablespoons **olive oil**

13 oz can **chopped tomatoes**

6 tablespoons **dry white wine**

Filling

2 teaspoons **olive oil**

1 small **onion**, finely chopped

2 **anchovy fillets in olive oil**, drained and roughly chopped

2 **garlic cloves**, crushed

2 cups **fresh white bread crumbs**

2 tablespoons roughly chopped **flat-leaf parsley**, plus extra to garnish

large pinch of **dried red pepper flakes**

salt

Pull the squid wings away from the body cavities. Roughly chop the wings and the tentacles and set aside.

For the filling, heat the oil in a skillet over a medium heat. Add the onion and anchovies and cook for 8 minutes until the onion is soft and translucent. Stir in the chopped squid and garlic and cook, stirring, for 1 minute. Let cool, then stir in the remaining filling ingredients.

Stuff the squid body cavities with the filling, using a teaspoon to help push the filling in. Fill only three-quarters of the way up, then secure the ends with toothpicks.

Heat the oil in a large, heavy skillet over a high heat. Add the squid and cook for 1–2 minutes on each side until golden brown. Pour in the tomatoes and wine and bring to a boil. Reduce the heat and simmer for 25–30 minutes until the sauce has thickened and the squid is so tender that it offers no resistance when pricked with a fork. Serve garnished with chopped parsley, accompanied by steamed potatoes or soft polenta.

For barbecued stuffed squid, stuff the squid as above, also adding 1 tablespoon chopped mint and the finely grated zest of 1 lemon to the filling. Cook over a gas barbecue preheated to high or over a charcoal barbecue with coals covered with a thin layer of gray ash for 3–4 minutes on each side. Serve with a squeeze of lemon and a drizzle of extra virgin olive oil.

fried calamari

Serves **4**
Preparation time **15 minutes**
Cooking time **10 minutes**

2 lb **squid**, cleaned
(see page 14)
vegetable oil, for deep-frying
¾ cup **all-purpose flour**
salt
lemon wedges, to serve

Cut the squid bodies into rings. Dry the rings and the tentacles thoroughly with paper towels.

Heat enough oil for deep-frying in a deep saucepan to 350–375°F, or until a cube of bread browns in 30 seconds. Season the squid with salt, then coat half in the flour, shaking off any excess. Add to the hot oil and cook for 2–3 minutes, or until golden and crisp. Remove with a slotted spoon and drain on paper towels. Sprinkle with a pinch of salt. Repeat with the remaining squid. Serve immediately with lemon wedges.

For spicy fried shrimp, replace the squid with 20 raw peeled jumbo shrimp. Mix ¼ teaspoon cayenne pepper into 1 cup all-purpose flour and make into a batter by stirring in ¾ cup ice-cold sparkling water. Season the shrimp with salt, then coat in the batter and deep-fry in batches, as above, for 4–5 minutes. Drain on paper towels and serve with lemon wedges.

meat
& poultry

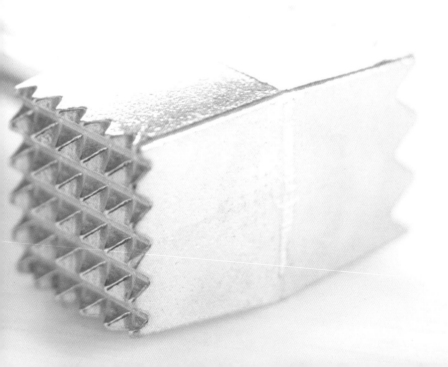

classic meatloaf

Serves **4**
Preparation time **25 minutes**
Cooking time **55 minutes**

2 thick slices of **white bread**,
    crusts removed and broken
    into chunks
2 tablespoons **milk**
large pinch of freshly
    grated **nutmeg**
1 lb **ground beef**
6 slices of **pancetta** or **bacon**,
    finely chopped
1 small **onion**, finely chopped
3 **garlic cloves**, finely chopped
4 tablespoons freshly grated
    Parmesan cheese
1 **egg**, lightly beaten
1 cup **fine dry white bread**
    crumbs
2 tablespoons **olive oil**
⅔ cup **dry white wine**
13 oz can **chopped tomatoes**
finely grated **zest** of 1 **orange**
2 tablespoons roughly
    chopped **flat-leaf parsley**
salt and **pepper**

Soak the bread in a bowl with the milk and nutmeg for about 10 minutes until the milk is absorbed. Mash with a fork. Combine the beef, pancetta or bacon, onion, and half the garlic in a large bowl. Add the Parmesan, egg, and bread. Season with salt and pepper. Mix gently with your hands until well combined. Form into a loaf shape. Spread the bread crumbs out on a large plate and roll the meatloaf over to coat thoroughly.

Heat the oil in a shallow saucepan with a tight-fitting lid over a medium heat. Add the meatloaf and cook, turning occasionally, until golden all over. Add the wine, boil rapidly until reduced by half, then add the tomatoes. Cover and simmer very gently, turning the meatloaf occasionally and adding a little water if necessary, for 40–45 minutes, or until a knife inserted into the center comes out hot.

Lift onto a serving dish. Stir the orange zest, parsley, and remaining garlic into the pan and simmer for 2 minutes. Season with salt and pepper. Spoon over the meatloaf.

For meatballs in red wine sauce, soak the bread, then combine the remaining ingredients as above, omitting the bread crumbs, oil, wine, and tomatoes. Season and shape into golf-ball size balls. Heat 2 tablespoons olive oil in a skillet over a medium heat, add the meatballs, and cook for 8–10 minutes until golden. Add ¾ cup full-bodied red wine, boil for 2 minutes, then stir in the tomatoes. Bring to a boil, then simmer, covered, for 20 minutes.

calf's liver & caramelized onions

Serves **4**

Preparation time **10 minutes**

Cooking time **40–45 minutes**

¼ cup **butter**

2 tablespoons **olive oil**

2 large **onions**, thinly sliced

1¼ lb **calf's liver**, thinly sliced
(ask your butcher to slice as
thinly as possible)

2 tablespoons finely chopped
flat-leaf parsley

salt and **pepper**

Melt half the butter with the oil in a large skillet with a tight-fitting lid. Add the onions and season with salt and pepper, then cover and cook over a very low heat, stirring occasionally, for 35–40 minutes until very soft and golden. Remove to a bowl and increase the heat under the pan to high.

Season the liver with salt and pepper and melt the remaining butter in the pan. Once the butter starts foaming, add the liver and cook for 1–2 minutes until browned. Turn over and return the onions to the pan. Cook for a minute more, then serve immediately with the parsley sprinkled over.

For chicken liver & caramelized onions, cook the onions as above and remove from the pan. Replace the calf's liver with 13 oz chicken livers, coated in seasoned flour. Cook the livers in the remaining butter in the pan as above for 4–5 minutes, turning once. Add 1 tablespoon aged balsamic vinegar, swirl in the pan for a couple of seconds, then return the caramelized onions to the pan. Cook for a minute more, stir in the parsley as above and serve immediately.

roast lamb with wine & juniper

Serves **6**

Preparation time **20 minutes**

Cooking time **1 hour
35 minutes**

2 tablespoons **olive oil**

1 **leg of lamb**, about 3 lb,
trimmed of excess fat

10 **juniper berries**, crushed

3 **garlic cloves**, crushed

2 oz **salted anchovies**, boned
and rinsed

1 tablespoon chopped
rosemary

2 tablespoons **balsamic
vinegar**

2 **rosemary sprigs**

1 ¼ cups **dry white wine**

salt and **pepper**

Heat the oil in a roasting pan in which the lamb will fit snugly. Add the lamb and cook until browned all over. Allow to cool.

Pound 6 of the juniper berries, the garlic, anchovies, and chopped rosemary with the end of a rolling pin in a bowl. Stir in the vinegar and mix to a paste. Make small incisions all over the lamb with a small, sharp knife. Spread the paste over the lamb, working it into the incisions. Season with salt and pepper. Put the rosemary sprigs in the roasting pan and put the lamb on top. Pour in the wine and add the remaining juniper berries.

Cover the roasting pan with foil and bring to a boil, then cook in a preheated oven, 325°F, for 1 hour, turning the lamb every 20 minutes. Raise the temperature to 400°F, uncover and roast for an additional 30 minutes until the lamb is very tender.

For leg of lamb with lemon & rosemary, omit the juniper berries and pound the grated zest of 2 lemons, with the garlic, anchovies, and rosemary. Replace the vinegar with the juice of 1 lemon. Spoon the sauce over the lamb, as above.

veal scallops with prosciutto

Serves **4**
Preparation time **10 minutes**
Cooking time **10 minutes**

4 **veal scallops**, about
   5 oz each
4 slices of **prosciutto**
4 **sage leaves**
all-purpose flour, for dusting
2 tablespoons **butter**
2 tablespoons **olive oil**
⅔ cup **dry white wine**
salt and **pepper**

Lay the scallops between 2 sheets of plastic wrap and beat with a rolling pin until wafer thin.

Season with salt and pepper, then lay a slice of prosciutto on each scallop, followed by a sage leaf. Secure the sage and ham in position with a toothpick, then lightly dust both sides of the veal with flour. Season again with salt and pepper.

Melt the butter with the oil in a large skillet over a high heat. Add the scallops and cook for 2–3 minutes on each side until golden brown. Add the wine to the pan and bubble until thickened and reduced by about half. Serve immediately, accompanied by boiled or steamed potatoes and/or a cooked green vegetable.

For chicken breast with rosemary & pancetta, replace the veal with 4 boneless chicken breasts, about 5 oz each, skinned. Top each flattened breast with a sprinkling of rosemary needles, then wrap each in a slice of pancetta, in place of the prosciutto, omitting the sage. Dust with flour, season with salt and pepper, and cook as above.

pork braised in milk

Serves **6**

Preparation time **10 minutes**,
plus resting

Cooking time 1¾ **hours**

2 tablespoons **butter**

3 tablespoons **olive oil**

1 **loin of pork with 6 chops**,
about 4½ lb in total, chined
and skin removed (ask your
butcher to do this for you)

4 cups **milk**

4 **garlic cloves**, peeled but
kept whole

pared **rind** of 2 **lemons**

8 **sage leaves**

salt and **pepper**

Melt the butter with the oil in a large, heavy flameproof casserole or a roasting pan large enough to hold the pork. Season the pork with salt and pepper and add to the pan, fat-side down. Cook over a medium-high heat for 10 minutes until golden brown.

Pour away most of the fat and turn the pork over, skin-side up. Pour in the milk and add the garlic, lemon rind, and sage. Bring to a boil, then cover with a lid or foil, leaving a little gap for the steam to escape. Cook on the burner over a very low heat or in a preheated oven, 300°F, for 1½ hours, basting regularly with the sauce. The pork is ready when the meat feels very tender when pierced with a fork.

Remove the meat and allow to rest for 10 minutes. The sauce, which should be straw color, will be unattractively lumpy, so vigorously beat to break up the lumps or process in a food processor or blender until smooth. Reheat if necessary and season with salt and pepper. Separate the loin into 6 chops and serve with the sauce spooned over.

For lamb shanks braised in milk, replace the pork with 6 lamb shanks and cook as above, using 3 rosemary sprigs instead of the sage leaves. Add a generous grating of nutmeg to the sauce before beating or blending away the lumps.

160

lamb chops with red pesto

Serves **4**
Preparation time **15 minutes**,
plus marinating
Cooking time **4–6 minutes**

12 **lamb chops**, each
approximately 4 oz
2 tablespoons **olive oil**
juice of ½ **lemon**
1 **garlic clove**, crushed
2 **rosemary sprigs**, roughly
chopped
salt and **pepper**

Pesto
1 cup **sunblush tomatoes**
¾ cup **bottled roasted sweet
peppers**
⅓ cup **blanched almonds**
½ **red chili**, halved and seeded
2 **garlic cloves**, crushed
3 tablespoons freshly grated
Parmesan cheese
3 tablespoons **extra virgin
olive oil**

Put the chops in a bowl with the oil, lemon juice, garlic, and rosemary and toss well to combine. Cover and allow to marinate in the refrigerator for at least 1 hour or up to overnight.

Meanwhile, for the pesto, put the tomatoes, peppers, almonds, chili, and garlic in a food processor and process to a paste. Stir in the Parmesan and oil and season with salt.

Season the marinated chops with salt and pepper. Heat a ridged griddle pan over a high heat until smoking hot, or preheat a gas barbecue to high or, if using a charcoal barbecue, get the coals to the stage where there are no more flames and the coals are covered with a thin layer of gray ash. Add the chops and cook for 2–3 minutes on each side, depending on whether you like your lamb pink in the center or well done. Serve with the red pesto on the side.

For a steak sandwich with red pesto, replace the lamb with 1 lb tenderloin steak. Marinate and cook as above, then slice. Meanwhile, make the red pesto as above. Cut 4 ciabatta rolls open and drizzle the inside with olive oil. Griddle or barbecue for a few seconds to char slightly. Put the beef slices in the rolls and top with wild arugula leaves, red pesto, and a few slices of red onion.

deviled tenderloin steaks

Serves **4**
Preparation time **10 minutes**
Cooking time **10 minutes**

2 tablespoons **olive oil**
4 **tenderloin steaks**, about
  6 oz each
2 tablespoons **balsamic**
  vinegar
5 tablespoons **full-bodied**
  red wine
4 tablespoons **beef stock**
2 **garlic cloves**, chopped
1 teaspoon crushed
  fennel seeds
1 tablespoon **sundried**
  tomato paste
½ teaspoon **dried red pepper**
  flakes
salt and **pepper**

To garnish
chopped **flat-leaf parsley**
wild arugula leaves (optional)

Heat the oil in a nonstick skillet until smoking hot. Add the steaks and cook over a very high heat for about 2 minutes on each side, if you want your steaks to be medium rare. Remove to a plate, season with salt and pepper, and keep warm in a low oven.

Pour the vinegar, wine, and stock into the pan and boil for 30 seconds, scraping any sediment from the base of the pan. Add the garlic and fennel seeds and beat in the sundried tomato paste and pepper flakes. Bring the sauce to a boil and boil fast to reduce until syrupy.

Transfer the steaks to warmed serving plates, pouring any collected meat juices into the sauce. Return the sauce to a boil, then season with salt and pepper.

Pour the sauce over the steaks and serve immediately, garnished with chopped parsley and wild arugula leaves, if desired. Slice the steaks before serving, if you wish.

For deviled chicken breasts, heat the oil and use to cook 4 skinned chicken breasts for 5 minutes on each side. Leaving the chicken in the pan, follow the recipe above, replacing the beef stock with 4 tablespoons chicken stock and using ½ teaspoon dried oregano instead of the fennel seeds.

rabbit in white wine & rosemary

Serves **4–6**
Preparation time **15 minutes**
Cooking time **2 hours**

2 tablespoons **butter**
3 tablespoons **olive oil**
1 **rabbit**, about 3 lb, cut into
joints (ask your butcher to
do this for you)
2 **onions**, thinly sliced
1 small **celery stick**,
finely diced
pinch of **dried red pepper
flakes**
3 large **rosemary sprigs**
1 **lemon**, quartered
12 **black olives**
1½ cups **dry white wine**
1 cup **chicken stock**
salt

Melt half the butter with the oil in a large, flameproof casserole with a tight-fitting lid large enough to hold the rabbit in a single layer. Lightly season the rabbit with salt and add to the pan with the onions, celery, pepper flakes, and rosemary. Cover and cook over a low heat for 1½ hours, turning the rabbit pieces every 30 minutes.

Uncover the pan, increase the heat to high, and boil until most of the juices released by the rabbit during cooking have evaporated. Add the lemon and olives, stir well, then pour in the wine. Bring to a boil and boil for 2 minutes, for the alcohol to evaporate.

Pour in the stock and simmer, turning and basting the rabbit occasionally, for an additional 10–12 minutes until you have a rich, syrupy sauce. Serve hot.

For chicken with olives & rosemary, replace the rabbit with 1 chicken, cut into 8 joints (ask your butcher to do this). Put the chicken with all the remaining ingredients above in a large roasting pan and roast in a preheated oven, 400°F, for 1 hour, turning the chicken pieces occasionally, until the meat is tender and most of the juices have evaporated. Stir in 3 tablespoons cream and serve immediately.

roast herbed pork belly

Serves **4–6**

Preparation time **15 minutes**, plus resting

Cooking time **1 hour 50 minutes**

10 **sage leaves**

2 large **rosemary sprigs**

3 **garlic cloves**, crushed

1 tablespoon **fennel seeds**

4 tablespoons **olive oil**

1 **boned pork belly joint**, about 2½ lb

salt and **pepper**

Roughly chop the sage and rosemary and combine with the garlic, fennel seeds, and half the oil in a small bowl.

Place the pork on a cutting board, skin-side up, and score the rind at 1 inch intervals (with a very sharp knife). Turn the meat over, skin-side down, and season with salt and pepper. Rub the herb mixture all over the flesh. Roll the pork up and tie it tightly with string. Rub the skin all over with the remaining oil, then a generous amount of salt.

Roast in a preheated oven, 425°F, for 20 minutes, then reduce the temperature to 325°F, and roast for 1½ hours more. Allow the meat to rest for 10 minutes before carving and serving. The Braised Black Cabbage & Beans on page 198 or the Braised Artichokes & Potatoes on page 186 would make great accompaniments for the pork.

For sausage & apricot stuffed pork, instead of the herb mixture, roughly chop 4 sage leaves and 6 ready-to-eat dried apricots, then stir into 5 oz pork sausagemeat. Follow the recipe above from the second step onward, spreading the sausagement mixture over the seasoned pork.

beef in red wine

Serves **4**
Preparation time **10 minutes**
Cooking time **2¼ hours**

1¾ lb **brisket of beef**, cut
into 2 inch pieces
1 **celery stick**
2 **bay leaves**
3 cups **Barolo** or other full-
bodied red wine
1¼ cups **beef** or **chicken
stock**
2 **carrots**, cut at an angle
into 1½ inch slices
20 **baby onions**, peeled
but kept whole
salt and **pepper**

Season the beef with salt and pepper and put in a large, flameproof casserole with a tight-fitting lid. Add the celery and bay leaves, then pour in the wine and stock. Bring to a boil, then reduce the heat to a barely visible simmer and cook, covered, for 1½ hours, stirring occasionally.

Add the carrots and onions. Re-cover and simmer gently for an additional 45 minutes, adding a little water if the sauce becomes too thick.

Remove the beef from the heat and serve accompanied by mashed potatoes or soft polenta.

For oxtail in red wine with tomatoes, replace the beef with 4 lb oxtail chunks. Cook as above, adding a 13 oz can chopped tomatoes and reducing the red wine to 1½ cups. Simmer gently for 2½ hours. Oxtail releases a lot of fat, so ideally make the stew a day ahead, allow to cool completely, then refrigerate. Skim off the solidified layer of fat before reheating.

sausages & lentils in tomato sauce

Serves **4**

Preparation time **10 minutes**

Cooking time **1 hour 10 minutes**

3 tablespoons **olive oil**

8 **Italian pork sausages**

1 **onion**, roughly chopped

1 **celery stick**, roughly chopped

3 **garlic cloves**, crushed

¾ cup **full-bodied red wine**

13 oz can **chopped tomatoes**

5 cups **chicken stock**

1 **bay leaf**

1 **dried red chili**

½ cup **green lentils**

salt and **pepper**

extra virgin olive oil, for drizzling

Heat the oil in a large, heavy saucepan in which the sausages fit in a single layer. Add the sausages and cook over a medium heat for 10–12 minutes until golden brown all over. Remove and set aside.

Add the onion and celery to the pan and cook over a low heat for 8–10 minutes until softened. Stir in the garlic and cook for 2 minutes more.

Increase the heat to high, pour in the wine, and boil vigorously for 2 minutes, scraping any sediment from the base of the pan. Stir in the tomatoes, stock, bay leaf, and chili and bring to a boil. Add the lentils and return the sausages to the pan. Simmer gently for 40 minutes, or until the sausages and lentils are cooked through. Season with salt and pepper. Serve with a drizzle of extra virgin olive oil, accompanied by some crusty bread.

For cod & lentils in tomato sauce, omit the sausages and cook the other ingredients as above from the second step onward, finally adding the lentils to the pan. Once cooked until tender, add 4 cod fillets, about 4 oz each, to the pan and season with salt and pepper. Sprinkle with the grated zest of 1 lemon and 1 tablespoon chopped parsley, cover, and cook over a low heat for 10–12 minutes until cooked through.

chicken milanese

Serves **4**
Preparation time **20 minutes**
Cooking time **10–25 minutes**

4 **boneless chicken breasts**,
about 5–6 oz each, skinned
1 cup **all-purpose flour**
2 **eggs**, beaten
2 cups **dry white bread
crumbs**
3 tablespoons **flat-leaf
parsley**, chopped
5 tablespoons **olive oil**
salt and **pepper**
lemon wedges, to serve

Lay the chicken breasts between 2 sheets of plastic wrap and beat with a rolling pin until no more than ½ inch thick.

Put the flour, eggs, and bread crumbs in 3 separate dishes and season the flour and eggs with salt and pepper. Stir the chopped parsley into the bread crumbs. Turn each chicken breast in the flour, then dip into the eggs and coat in the bread crumbs.

Heat the oil in a skillet over a high heat. Add the flattened chicken breasts, 1 or 2 at a time, and cook for 2–3 minutes on each side until golden. Remove with a slotted spoon and drain on paper towels. Serve with lemon wedges, accompanied by a crisp green salad.

For turkey Milanese, replace the chicken with 4 turkey breast steaks, about 5–6 oz each, sliced ½ inch thick. For the coating, use 4 cups fresh white bread crumbs instead of the dry bread crumbs and flavor with 2 crushed garlic cloves, 2 tablespoons chopped flat-leaf parsley, and 1 tablespoon chopped thyme. Follow the recipe above.

roast chicken with herbs & garlic

Serves **4**
Preparation time **10 minutes**
Cooking time **about 1 hour**

8 **garlic cloves**, unpeeled
4 large **thyme sprigs**
3 large **rosemary sprigs**
1 **organic** or **free-range
  chicken**, about 3½ lb
1 tablespoon **olive oil**
salt and **pepper**

Put the garlic cloves and half the herb sprigs in the body cavity of the chicken. Pat the chicken dry with paper towels and rub the oil all over the outside of the bird. Strip the leaves off the remaining herb sprigs and rub over the bird, with a little salt and pepper.

Place the chicken, breast-side up, in a roasting pan. Roast in a preheated oven, 425°F, for 10 minutes. Turn the chicken over, breast-side down, reduce the oven temperature to 350°F, and cook for 20 minutes more. Finally, turn the chicken back to its original position and roast for another 25 minutes until the skin is crisp and golden. Check that the chicken is cooked by piercing the thigh with a knife. The juices should run clear, with no sign of pink. If not, cook for an additional 10 minutes.

Transfer to a warmed serving plate and let rest for 5 minutes before serving with the pan juices.

For roast chicken with lemon & sage, cut a lemon in half, then cut 1 half into slices. Carefully lift the skin covering the breast meat and ease in the lemon slices. Put the other lemon half in the body cavity with 8 sage leaves, in place of the thyme and rosemary sprigs, and the garlic as above. Roast as above.

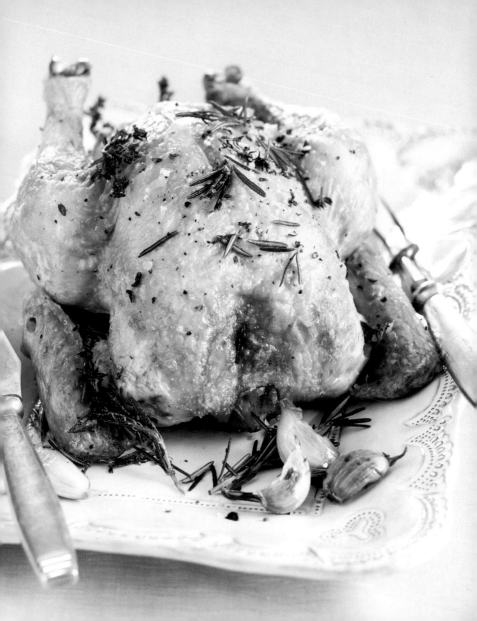

vegetables & legumes

eggplant & zucchini parmigiana

Serves **6**
Preparation time **15 minutes**
Cooking time **45–50 minutes**

2 cups **passata**
handful of **basil leaves**, torn
2 **garlic cloves**, crushed
4 tablespoons **olive oil**
2 lb **eggplants**, cut lengthwise
  into ½ inch slices
1 lb **zucchini**, cut lengthwise
  into ½ inch slices
10 oz **mozzarella cheese**
  (drained weight), chopped
1 cup freshly grated
  Parmesan cheese
salt and **pepper**

Combine the passata, basil, and garlic in a bowl, season with salt and pepper and stir in half the oil.

Toss the eggplants and zucchini in the remaining oil to coat. Heat a ridged griddle pan over a high heat until smoking hot. Add the vegetables, in batches, and cook for 2–3 minutes on each side until tender all the way through.

Spoon a little of the passata mixture onto the base of a deep baking dish, about 12 x 8 inches. Cover with a layer of mixed eggplant and zucchini, then sprinkle with some of the mozzarella. Spoon over 4 tablespoons of the passata mixture and scatter with Parmesan. Continue layering in this way until all the ingredients are used up, finishing with a layer of passata mixture and Parmesan.

Bake in a preheated oven, 350°F, for 25–30 minutes, or until golden and bubbly.

For fennel & olive parmigiana, replace the eggplants and zucchini with 4 fennel bulbs, cut lengthwise into ½ inch slices and 1 large onion, sliced into rings. Griddle and layer with the passata mixture and cheese as above, then top the final layer with a sprinkling of 15 pitted black olives. Bake as above.

broiled radicchio, fontina, & speck

Serves **4**
Preparation time **10 minutes**
Cooking time **15 minutes**

4 **radicchi di treviso** or
  2 **round radicchi**
2 tablespoons **olive oil**
8 slices of **speck**
3 oz **Fontina cheese**, thinly
  sliced
salt and **pepper**

Cut radicchio di treviso in half lengthwise. If using round radicchio, cut into quarters. Brush all sides of the radicchio with the oil, then season with salt and pepper. Arrange on a baking sheet and cook under a preheated medium broiler, about 5 inches from the heat source, for 10 minutes, until slightly softened. The leaves will darken in color, but they should not char, so reduce the heat or increase the distance between the radicchio and the heat source if necessary.

Drape each piece of radicchio with a slice of speck, then top with the Fontina. Broil for 2 minutes more until the cheese has melted and serve.

For broiled radicchio with walnut vinaigrette, first make the vinaigrette by beating together 1 tablespoon grainy mustard, 3 tablespoons walnut oil, and 2 tablespoons peanut oil in a bowl. Stir in 2 tablespoons roughly chopped walnuts and season with salt and pepper. Broil the radicchio as above, omitting the speck and cheese topping. Transfer to a serving bowl, spoon over the vinaigrette, and serve warm.

cannellini with sage & tomato

Serves **4**

Preparation time **10–15 minutes**, plus soaking (optional)

Cooking time **15 minutes** for canned beans; **45 minutes** for fresh; **1¾ hours** for dried

1½ cups shelled **fresh cannellini beans**, or 1 cup **dried cannellini beans**, soaked in cold water overnight, drained, and rinsed, or 2 x 13 oz cans **cannellini beans**, drained and rinsed

1 **bay leaf** (optional)

2 **garlic cloves**, unpeeled, or 1 garlic clove, chopped

2 teaspoons **olive oil**

1 **red onion**, thinly sliced

5 **sage leaves**, roughly chopped

pinch of **dried red pepper flakes**

2 **tomatoes**, skinned and chopped

salt

extra virgin olive oil, for drizzling (optional)

Put the fresh beans, if using, into a saucepan, pour in enough cold water to cover by about 2 inches and add the bay leaf and garlic cloves. Bring to a boil and skim off any scum that rises to the surface. Reduce the heat to a simmer and cook, uncovered, for 25–30 minutes, or until tender. Drain, reserving the garlic cloves. If using presoaked dried beans, cook as for the fresh beans, but they will take about 1½ hours to become tender. The canned beans are ready to use.

Heat the oil in a large, heavy skillet over a low heat. Add the onion, sage, and pepper flakes and cook, stirring occasionally, for 10 minutes until the onion is softened. If you cooked the beans from scratch, squeeze the garlic flesh out of the skins into the pan. If using canned beans, simply add the chopped garlic to the pan. Cook, stirring, for 1 minute, then add the beans and the tomatoes. Season with salt and cook, stirring, for 3–5 minutes. Serve drizzled with a little extra virgin olive oil, if desired.

For cannellini with pancetta & rosemary, prepare the beans following the first stage of the recipe above. Fry the onions and pepper flakes in olive oil as above, omitting the sage and adding 3 oz cubed pancetta and 1 large sprig of rosemary. Complete the recipe as above.

braised artichokes & potatoes

Serves **4**
Preparation time **30 minutes**
Cooking time **1 hour**

6 **baby globe artichokes**
juice of 1 **lemon**
4 tablespoons **olive oil**
2 **shallots**, thinly sliced
1 **garlic clove**, finely chopped
1 lb **potatoes**, peeled and cut
into 1 ½ inch chunks
⅔ cup shelled **fresh** or **frozen**
peas
handful of **flat-leaf parsley**,
roughly chopped
salt and **pepper**

Trim the stalks of the artichokes, leaving about 1 ¼ inches. Pull off and discard the tough outer leaves, exposing the paler tender leaves, then cut off their tips. Using a potato peeler, peel the stalk and dark green base until you see the lighter, yellowy flesh. Halve the artichokes and scoop out the hairy choke with a teaspoon and discard. Put in a bowl of cold water with the lemon juice to prevent discoloring.

Heat the oil in a large, heavy saucepan with a tight-fitting lid just large enough to hold the artichokes and potatoes in a single layer. Add the shallots and cook over a medium heat for 8–10 minutes until softened and translucent. Add the garlic and cook, stirring, for 1 minute. Toss in the drained artichokes, potatoes, and salt and pepper.

Pour in enough water to come a quarter of the way up the vegetables. Bring to a boil, then reduce to a slow simmer. Cover with waxed paper and the lid. Cook for 45 minutes. Stir in the peas and parsley and cook for an additional 5 minutes, or until the artichokes and potatoes are tender.

For braised zucchini, peas, & prosciutto, omit the artichokes and potatoes. Cut 3 oz prosciutto into thin strips and cook with the shallots as above. Once the garlic has cooked for 1 minute, stir in 2 zucchini, cut into ½ inch slices. Complete the recipe as above, but using 2 tablespoons chopped mint instead of the parsley.

sicilian caponata

Serves **4**
Preparation time **15 minutes**,
  plus standing
Cooking time **30 minutes**

6 tablespoons **olive oil**
2 **eggplants**, cut into 1½ inch
  cubes
1 large **onion**, coarsely
  chopped
3 **celery sticks**, sliced
⅓ cup **pine nuts**
2 **garlic cloves**, chopped
13 oz can **plum tomatoes**,
  drained and roughly chopped
2 tablespoons **capers in
  brine**, rinsed
⅓ cup **pitted green olives**
3 tablespoons **red wine
  vinegar**
1 tablespoon **superfine sugar**
6 **basil leaves**
salt and **pepper**

Heat the oil in a large skillet over a high heat until the oil begins to shimmer. Add the eggplants, in batches, and cook, stirring frequently, for 5–6 minutes until they are golden and tender. Use a slotted spoon to transfer to a bowl.

Pour away all but 2 tablespoons oil from the pan. Add the onion, celery, and pine nuts and cook over a low heat for 10 minutes until the vegetables are softened and lightly golden. Return the eggplants to the pan and stir in the remaining ingredients, except for the basil. Season with salt and pepper.

Bring the pan to a boil, then reduce the heat and simmer for 5 minutes. Stir in the basil. Remove from the heat and allow to stand for at least 15 minutes to allow the flavors to mingle. Serve warm or cold, as an antipasto, side dish, or as a vegetarian main course, with some bread on the side.

For potato & pepper caponata, peel and cut 1 lb potatoes into 1½ inch cubes. Cook in a saucepan of salted boiling water until tender, then drain. Omit the eggplant. Reduce the oil to 4 tablespoons and heat in a skillet. Add the onion, celery, and pine nuts with 2 red bell peppers, cored, seeded, and cut into large chunks, and cook as above. Toss in the potatoes and the remaining ingredients as above, but using black olives in place of the green. Season with salt and pepper, then follow the final step above to complete.

squash with mascarpone & sage

Serves **4**
Preparation time **15 minutes**
Cooking time **1 hour
10 minutes**

2 small **acorn squash**, each
about 1 lb
2 tablespoons **olive oil**
4 oz piece **smoked pancetta**,
diced
2 **garlic cloves**, crushed
2 tablespoons chopped **sage**,
plus extra, to garnish
¾ cup **mascarpone cheese**
4 **sundried tomatoes** in oil,
drained and chopped
2 tablespoons freshly grated
Parmesan cheese
salt and **pepper**

To serve
griddled **bread**
green salad

Cut the squash in half lengthwise and carefully scoop
out the seeds. Season the shells lightly with salt and
pepper and place, cut side up, in a roasting pan. Drizzle
with a little of the oil and bake in a preheated oven,
400°F, for 45 minutes.

Dry-fry the pancetta for about 5 minutes, until it is
golden and has released its fat. Lower the heat, add
the remaining oil, and gently fry the garlic and sage for
an additional 4–5 minutes, until the garlic is softened.

Remove the squash from the oven and fill the hollows
with the pancetta mixture. Spoon in the mascarpone
and sprinkle with the sundried tomatoes and Parmesan.
Return to the oven for 15–20 minutes, until bubbling
and golden. Garnish with sage leaves and serve with
some griddled bread and a crisp green salad.

For eggplants with pancetta & sage, cut 2 eggplants
in half lengthwise and roast instead of the squash, as
above. Follow step 2 and stir 3 tablespoons each fresh
white bread crumbs and grated Parmesan into the
pancetta mixture. Use to top the eggplants and bake
for an additional 15 minutes.

garlicky potatoes with tomatoes

Serves **4**
Preparation time **10 minutes**
Cooking time **1 hour**

1¼ lb **potatoes**, unpeeled
2 **onions**, thickly sliced
1 **garlic bulb**, broken
  into cloves
7 oz **cherry tomatoes**,
  on the vine
3 tablespoons **extra virgin
  olive oil**
⅔ cup **dry white wine**
1 teaspoon **dried oregano**
pared **rind** of 1 small **orange**
salt and **pepper**

Cut the potatoes in half lengthwise, then each half into 3 wedges. Put in a large roasting pan with all the remaining ingredients, season with salt and pepper, and stir well to combine thoroughly.

Roast in a preheated oven, 400°F, for 1 hour, or until the potatoes are cooked through. Stir the vegetables in the pan a couple of times during cooking. If the liquid dries out so much that the tomatoes and onions begin to stick to the base, add a little hot water to stop them burning.

For potatoes with red peppers & olives, prepare the potatoes and put in the roasting pan with the remaining ingredients as above, but omit the garlic, tomatoes, and orange rind. Toss in 2 red bell peppers, cored, seeded, and cut into 1 inch strips, season with salt and pepper, and roast as above for 50 minutes. Stir in ⅓ cup pitted black olives and roast for an additional 10 minutes. Stir in a handful of basil leaves.

peperonata

Serves **4**
Preparation time **10 minutes**,
plus preparing the peppers
Cooking time **45 minutes**

2 large **red bell peppers**,
broiled, skinned, cored, and
seeded (see page 46)
2 large **yellow bell peppers**,
broiled, skinned, cored, and
seeded (see page 46)
2 teaspoons **olive oil**
1 small **onion**, finely chopped
2 **garlic cloves**, finely chopped
13 oz can **plum tomatoes**,
roughly chopped
6 large **basil leaves**, torn
extra virgin olive oil, for
drizzling (optional)
salt

Cut the peppers into wide strips and set aside.

Heat the oil in a heavy saucepan over a low heat. Add the onion and cook, stirring occasionally, for 10 minutes. Add the garlic and cook, stirring, for 1 minute. Add the tomatoes and their juice and the pepper strips. Season with salt and bring to a boil. Reduce the heat to a gentle simmer and cook, stirring occasionally, for 25 minutes.

Stir the basil into the pan and cook for an additional 5–10 minutes until the sauce has reduced. Drizzle with extra virgin olive oil before serving, if desired. Serve immediately as a side dish, or spoon over soft polenta or stir into pasta. Alternatively, serve cold as an antipasto.

For caper & lemon peperonata, follow the recipe as above also adding 2 tablespoons capers and the grated zest of 1 lemon to the pan with the basil.

spinach & pea frittata

Serves **4**

Preparation time **10 minutes**

Cooking time **25 minutes**

1 tablespoon **olive oil**

1 **onion**, thinly sliced

3 cups **baby spinach**

1 cup shelled **fresh** or
   frozen peas

6 **eggs**

salt and **pepper**

Heat the oil in a heavy, ovenproof, nonstick 9 inch skillet over a low heat. Add the onion and cook for 6–8 minutes until softened, then stir in the spinach and peas and cook for another 2 minutes, or until any moisture released by the spinach has evaporated.

Beat the eggs in a bowl and season lightly with salt and pepper. Stir in the cooked vegetables, then pour the mixture into the pan and quickly arrange the vegetables so that they are evenly dispersed. Cook over a low heat for 8–10 minutes, or until all but the top of the frittata is set.

Transfer the pan to a preheated very hot broiler and cook about 4 inches from the heat source until the top is set but not browned. Give the pan a shake to loosen the frittata, then transfer to a plate to cool. Serve slightly warm or at room temperature, accompanied by a green salad.

For zucchini, pea, & cheese frittata, follow the first step above, but replace the spinach with 1 large zucchini, coarsely grated. Add 4 tablespoons freshly grated Parmesan cheese and 4 oz cubed mozzarella cheese to the raw egg mixture with the vegetables and cook as above.

braised black cabbage & beans

Serves **4**

Preparation time **10 minutes**

Cooking time **30 minutes**

3 lb **cavolo nero (black cabbage)**

3 tablespoons **olive oil**

2 **garlic cloves**, thinly sliced

1/4 teaspoon **dried red pepper flakes**

13 oz can **cranberry beans**, drained and rinsed

salt

Remove the thick stalks of the cabbage by holding the stems with one hand and using the other hand to strip away the leaves. Discard the stalks. Cook the leaves in a saucepan of boiling water for 15 minutes until just tender, then drain thoroughly.

Heat the oil in a large skillet over a low heat. Add the garlic, pepper flakes and cranberry beans and cook for 5 minutes, then stir in the cooked cabbage. Season with salt and cook, stirring, for 6–8 minutes until the cabbage has completely wilted and absorbed the flavors. Serve immediately.

For spinach with pine nuts, follow the recipe above from the second step onward, replacing the cranberry beans with 1/3 cup pine nuts. Use 1 lb baby spinach, instead of the cabbage, toss into the pan raw and cook, stirring, for 2–3 minutes until wilted. Stir a light grating of nutmeg into the cooked spinach before serving.

potato & green bean bake

Serves **4**
Preparation time **10 minutes**
Cooking time **45 minutes**

1 lb **floury potatoes**, peeled
  and cut into large chunks
10 oz **green beans**, trimmed
  and halved
2 **garlic cloves**, finely chopped
handful of **basil leaves**, torn
1 cup freshly grated
  Parmesan cheese
1 cup **ricotta cheese**
3 **eggs**, lightly beaten
2 cups **fresh white bread
  crumbs**
2 tablespoons **olive oil**, plus
  extra for oiling
salt and **pepper**

Simmer the potatoes in a saucepan of salted boiling water for 10 minutes, then add the beans and cook for an additional 3–4 minutes until the potatoes are cooked through and the beans are just tender. Drain, return to the pan, and mash to a lumpy puree.

Stir the garlic, basil, cheeses, and eggs into the vegetable puree and season with salt and pepper.

Sprinkle an oiled cake pan or ovenproof dish with a thin layer of the bread crumbs. Pile in the vegetable mash, sprinkle with the remaining bread crumbs, and drizzle with the oil. Bake in a preheated oven, 400°F, for 25–30 minutes until the topping is crisp and golden.

For potato, olive, & sunblush tomato bake, cook the potatoes and mash as above, but omit the beans. Stir the garlic, eggs, and cheeses into the mash as above together with ⅓ cup roughly chopped pitted black olives and 8 roughly chopped sunblush tomatoes, replacing the basil with ½ teaspoon dried oregano. Follow the final step above to complete.

desserts

lemon panna cotta & raspberries

Serves **6**

Preparation time **10 minutes**, plus chilling and marinating

Cooking time **5 minutes**

2½ cups **heavy cream**
½ cup **superfine sugar**
pared **rind** of 2 **lemons**
1 **vanilla bean**, split lengthwise and seeds removed
1½ cups **milk**
3 teaspoons **powdered gelatin**
1 cup **fresh raspberries**
5 **mint leaves**, roughly chopped
3 tablespoons **grappa**

Put the cream, sugar, lemon rind, and vanilla seeds in a saucepan. Bring to a boil over a low heat, then remove from the heat and allow to infuse for 5 minutes.

Meanwhile, bring the milk to a boil in a separate saucepan. Remove from the heat and carefully sprinkle with the gelatin, in as thin and even a layer as you can manage. Allow to stand for 2–3 minutes until the gelatin no longer looks dry, then stir to dissolve.

Strain the infused cream through a sieve into the milk and pour the mixture into 6 x ¾ cup dariole molds. Cover each with plastic wrap and chill for at least 5 hours until set. It will keep for up to 3 days in the refrigerator.

Combine the raspberries, mint, and grappa in a bowl. Cover and allow to marinate at room temperature for 30 minutes and up to 4 hours.

Unmold the panna cotta by carefully dipping the base and sides of the molds in warm water for a few seconds. Invert onto individual serving plates and serve with the marinated raspberries.

For coffee-cream liqueur panna cotta, omit the lemon rind and the first step above. Dissolve the gelatin in the milk, as in the second step, then stir in 1¼ cups each coffee-flavored cream liqueur and heavy cream. Pour into the dariole molds and chill as above. Instead of the marinated raspberries, serve with the coffee sauce on page 216.

apricot jelly tart

Serves **6–8**

Preparation time **20 minutes**, plus chilling

Cooking time **20–25 minutes**

2¼ cups **all-purpose flour**, plus extra for dusting

⅓ cup **superfine sugar**

½ cup **unsalted butter**, diced

1 **egg** and 1 **egg yolk**, lightly beaten

¾ cup **low-sugar apricot jelly**

confectioners' sugar, for dusting

Put the flour and superfine sugar in a bowl, add the butter and blend in with your fingertips until the mixture resembles coarse bread crumbs. Gradually mix in enough of the eggs to bring the pastry together. Knead very lightly into a dough. Cover with plastic wrap and chill for 30–45 minutes.

Roll two-thirds of the pastry out on a lightly floured work surface. Use to line a shallow, 9 inch fluted tart pan, then fill with the jelly. Roll the remaining pastry out to a thickness of about ¼ inch, then cut strips about ½ inch wide. Lightly brush the rim of the pastry shell with water. Arrange the pastry strips in a lattice pattern over the tart. Chill for 20 minutes until firm.

Bake on a baking sheet in a preheated oven, 400°F, for 20–25 minutes until the pastry is firm and golden. Allow to cool on a wire rack, then remove from the pan and serve with a generous dusting of confectioners' sugar. The tart will keep in an airtight container for up to 2 days.

For chocolate & raspberry jelly tart, reduce the quantity of flour in the pastry to 1¾ cups and stir in ¾ cup cocoa powder with the sugar before blending in the butter. Use the pastry to line the pan as above, then fill with ¾ cup low-sugar raspberry jelly instead of the apricot. Finish the tart and bake as above.

chocolate & hazelnut parfaits

Serves **6**

Preparation time **20 minutes**,
  plus cooling and freezing

Cooking time **5–10 minutes**

1 cup **blanched hazelnuts**

4 oz **bittersweet chocolate
with 70% cocoa solids**,
  broken into pieces, plus extra
  chocolate curls to decorate

2½ cups **heavy cream**

2 **eggs**, separated

1½ cups **confectioners' sugar**

cocoa powder, to decorate

Spread the hazelnuts out on a baking sheet and toast in a preheated oven, 325°F, for 5–10 minutes until golden. Allow to cool completely, then grind very finely.

Put the chocolate in a heatproof bowl set over a saucepan of hot water and allow to melt. Whip the cream in a bowl until it holds its shape, then fold in the nuts. Beat the egg yolks in a large bowl with 2 tablespoons of the confectioners' sugar until pale and creamy. Beat the egg whites in a separate bowl until soft peaks form, then add the remaining confectioners' sugar, spoonful by spoonful, beating well after each addition, until the mixture is very thick.

Stir the melted chocolate into the egg yolk mixture. Fold in the cream mixture, then the meringue mixture. Turn into 6 x ¾ cup molds and freeze for 6 hours until firm.

Transfer to the refrigerator for 10 minutes before serving to soften slightly. Decorate with chocolate curls and dust with cocoa powder. Serve with dessert cookies.

For chocolate, almond, & prune parfaits, replace the hazelnuts with blanched almonds and prepare as above. Roughly chop 6 prunes and soak in 3 tablespoons of grappa for 30 minutes. Follow the recipe above, folding in the prunes just before turning the mixture into the molds. Complete as above.

lemon & ricotta tart

Serves **8–10**

Preparation time **15 minutes**, plus chilling

Cooking time **50–55 minutes**

12 oz **ready-made sweet short pastry**

all-purpose flour, for dusting

4 **eggs**

½ cup **superfine sugar**

1 ½ cups **ricotta cheese**

1 ¾ cups **heavy cream**

zest and **juice** of 3 **lemons**

fresh berries, to decorate

Roll the pastry out on a lightly floured work surface. Use to line a 9 inch fluted tart pan, then chill for 10 minutes. Line the pastry shell with waxed paper and fill with pie weights.

Bake the pastry shell in a preheated oven, 350°F, for 10 minutes. Remove the pie weights and paper and bake for another 5 minutes until golden.

Beat the remaining ingredients together in a bowl and use to fill the pastry shell. Reduce the oven temperature to 300°F, and bake the tart for 35–40 minutes until just set. Serve with fresh berries, such as strawberries and blueberries, and a generous dusting of confectioners' sugar.

For chocolate & ricotta tart, make and bake the pastry shell as above. Then make the filling as above, but omit the lemon zest and juice and increase the heavy cream to 2 cups. Stir in 4 oz roughly chopped bittersweet chocolate. Use to fill the pastry shell and bake as above.

pear & almond cake

Serves **8**
Preparation time **20 minutes**
Cooking time **35 minutes**

½ cup **unsalted butter**,
  softened, plus extra for
  greasing
½ cup **superfine sugar**
2 large **eggs**, beaten
½ cup **all-purpose flour**,
  sifted
1 cup **ground almonds**
½ teaspoon **baking powder**
3 **ripe pears**, peeled, halved,
  and cored
½ cup **slivered almonds**
confectioners' sugar, for
  dusting

Beat the butter and superfine sugar together in a bowl until pale and fluffy. Add the eggs, a little at a time, beating well after each addition. If the mixture starts to curdle, add 1 tablespoon of the flour. Fold in the flour, ground almonds, and baking powder using a large metal spoon and tip into a greased 8 inch springform cake pan and use a spatula to even out the mixture.

Arrange the pear halves over the top of the cake and bake in a preheated oven, 375°F, for 25 minutes. Sprinkle the slivered almonds over the top and return to the oven for an additional 10 minutes. The cake is ready when a skewer inserted into the center of the cake comes out clean.

Allow the cake to cool in the pan, then carefully remove the ring and base. Dust with confectioners' sugar before serving with Mascarpone, Marsala, & Orange Cream (see below), if desired.

For mascarpone, Marsala, & orange cream, to serve as an accompaniment, beat the grated zest of 1 orange and 2 tablespoons of its juice in a bowl with 2 tablespoons sweet Marsala and ½ cup mascarpone cheese. Sweeten with confectioners' sugar to taste.

caramel panna cotta & apricots

Serves **4**

Preparation time **30 minutes**, plus standing, cooling, and chilling

Cooking time **15 minutes**

2½ cups **heavy cream**

½ cup **superfine sugar**

1 **vanilla bean**, split lengthwise

⅓ cup **granulated sugar**

2 tablespoons **water**

4 tablespoons **milk**

1 tablespoon **powdered gelatin**

Apricots

8 **ripe apricots**, halved, pitted, and cut into thirds

⅔ cup **water**

⅓ cup **superfine sugar**

1 **vanilla bean**, split lengthwise

Put the cream, superfine sugar, and vanilla bean in a saucepan and heat until just below boiling point, stirring occasionally. Remove from the heat and allow to infuse for 20 minutes.

Meanwhile, heat the granulated sugar in the measurement water in a heavy saucepan until it has dissolved, then boil until the syrup turns to a golden caramel. Quickly pour into 4 x ⅔ cup ramekins or small molds. Set on a tray and leave to harden.

Pour the milk into a small saucepan and sprinkle on the gelatin. Warm over a low heat until the gelatin dissolves. Stir into the infused cream mixture. Bring to a boil, then immediately remove from the heat and strain through a sieve into a pitcher. Pour into the ramekins or molds. Allow to cool for at least 5 hours, until set.

Put the apricots in a small saucepan with the measurement water, sugar, and vanilla bean. Bring slowly to a boil, then cover and simmer gently for 5–8 minutes until just tender. Allow to cool, then remove the vanilla bean, cover, and chill.

Carefully loosen the panna cottas and turn out onto individual serving plates. Serve with the apricots.

For citron panna cotta, sprinkle ⅓ cup chopped candied citron over the set caramel, before filling the ramekins or molds with the panna cotta mixture. Omit the apricot sauce and serve instead with a drizzle of Limoncello liqueur.

zabaglione semifreddo with coffee

Serves **6**
Preparation time **15 minutes**,
  plus freezing
Cooking time **10 minutes**

6 **egg yolks**
½ cup **superfine sugar**
6 tablespoons **sweet Marsala**
1¼ cups **heavy cream**
30 **ladyfingers**

Coffee sauce
¾ cup **cold espresso coffee**
½ cup **granulated sugar**
3 tablespoons **coffee-flavored
  liqueur**

Beat the egg yolks with the superfine sugar in a heatproof bowl set over a saucepan of gently simmering water until the sugar has melted. Add the Marsala and continue beating for another 6–8 minutes, or until the mixture has thickened and holds its shape.

Whip the cream in a bowl until soft peaks form. Gently fold in the egg mixture. Roughly break the ladyfingers, then fold into the zabaglione. Tip into a 2 lb loaf pan lined with plastic wrap. Cover with plastic wrap and freeze for at least 6 hours or overnight until set.

Make the coffee sauce. Heat the coffee in a small saucepan, add the granulated sugar and stir until melted. Add the liqueur and boil vigorously until the sauce becomes thick and syrupy.

Turn the semifreddo out onto a serving plate and spoon over the sauce, which can be warm or at room temperature. Serve cut into slices.

For individual zabaglione semifreddos with raspberry sauce, make the zabaglione mixture as above and set in 6 dariole molds lined with plastic wrap. In place of the coffee sauce, heat 1¼ cups raspberries in a small saucepan with 1 tablespoon superfine sugar and 3 tablespoons apple juice. Bring to a boil, then simmer gently for 2 minutes. Crush the berries with the back of a fork and squeeze in the juice of ½ lemon. Invert the semifreddos onto individual plates and serve with the sauce.

almond cookies

Makes about **14**
Preparation time **20 minutes**
Cooking time **10 minutes**

1 ¼ cups **ground almonds**
1 tablespoon **all-purpose flour**
¾ cup **superfine sugar**, plus extra for coating
½ teaspoon **baking powder**
1 **egg white**
½ teaspoon **vanilla extract**

Combine the almonds, flour, sugar, and baking powder in a large bowl. Beat the egg white in a separate bowl until it holds its shape and has a consistency resembling shaving foam. Fold into the almond mixture. Add the vanilla extract and stir to combine thoroughly.

Dust a work surface with sugar. Roll 1 tablespoon of the cookie dough in the palm of your hands to make a sausage shape about 2½ inches long. Roll in the sugar, then place on a baking sheet lined with parchment paper. Repeat with the remaining dough to make about 14 cookies. Make sure you leave plenty of space between each cookie, as they spread during cooking.

Bake the cookies in a preheated oven, 400°F, for 10 minutes until lightly golden.

For candied fruit & raisin cookies, prepare the cookie dough as above, but reduce the superfine sugar to ⅔ cup and stir in 2 tablespoons chopped candied peel, and 2 tablespoons golden raisins with the vanilla extract. Shape into rolls, coat, and bake as above.

chocolate sorbet

Makes about **3¾ cups**
Preparation time **15 minutes**,
plus chilling and freezing
Cooking time **10 minutes**

2½ cups **water**
⅔ cup **dark brown sugar**
1 cup **granulated sugar**
½ cup **unsweetened cocoa
powder**
1 oz **bittersweet chocolate
with 70% cocoa solids**,
finely chopped
2½ teaspoons **vanilla extract**
1 teaspoon **instant espresso
coffee powder**

Put the measurement water, sugars, and cocoa powder
in a saucepan and mix together. Heat gently, stirring
until the sugar has dissolved. Increase the heat to
bring the mixture to a boil, then reduce to a simmer for
8 minutes.

Remove the pan from the heat and stir in the
chocolate, vanilla extract, and espresso powder until
thoroughly dissolved. Pour into a bowl and cool over ice
or allow to cool and chill.

Freeze in an ice-cream machine according to the
manufacturer's instructions. Serve immediately or
transfer to a chilled plastic freezerproof container and
store in the freezer for up to 1 month. If you are using
the sorbet straight from the freezer, transfer to the
refrigerator 20 minutes before serving to soften slightly.

For rum & chocolate-chip sorbet, replace the vanilla
extract with 3 tablespoons dark rum. Stir 3 oz chopped
bittersweet chocolate into the ice-cream mixture
before churning.

classic tiramisu

Serves **4**

Preparation time **20 minutes**, plus chilling

3 **eggs**, separated
½ cup **superfine sugar**
1 cup **mascarpone cheese**
¾ cup **cold espresso coffee**
4 tablespoons **sweet Marsala**
32–34 **ladyfingers**
3 oz **semisweet chocolate**, grated

Beat the egg yolks and sugar in a bowl with a hand-held electric mixer until light, airy, and the beaters leave a trail when lifted. Put the mascarpone in a large bowl and beat in one-third of the egg mixture until smooth, then fold in the remaining egg mixture. Beat the egg whites in a separate bowl until they hold their shape and have a consistency resembling shaving foam. Fold into the mascarpone mixture.

Pour the coffee and Marsala into a shallow bowl and dip in the ladyfingers until soaked on both sides but not all the way through. Arrange a layer of tightly packed ladyfingers in four 4 inch bowls. Spread with half the mascarpone mixture, then top with a second layer of soaked ladyfingers. Use the remaining mascarpone mixture to cover the ladyfingers. Cover with plastic wrap and chill for at least 3 hours or up to overnight.

Just before serving, remove the tiramisu from the refrigerator and dust with the grated chocolate.

For blackberry & lemon tiramisu, make the mascarpone mixture as above, but add 1 cup crushed blackberries and the finely grated zest of 1 lemon at the end of the first step. Complete the recipe as above, but decorate the top with blackberries before dusting with grated chocolate.

panettone

Serves **8**
Preparation time **25 minutes**,
  plus rising
Cooking time **55 minutes**

1 tablespoon **active dry yeast**
²⁄₃ cup warm **milk**
about 4 cups **white bread
  flour**, plus extra for dusting
2 teaspoons **salt**
1 **egg**, plus 4 **egg yolks**
¹⁄₃ cup **superfine sugar**
finely grated zest of 1 **lemon**
finely grated zest of 1 **orange**
³⁄₄ cup **unsalted butter**,
  softened
¹⁄₃ cup **candied orange** and
  lemon peel
³⁄₄ cup **raisins**

Line a deep 6½ inch cake pan with a double strip of nonstick parchment paper which projects 5 inches above the rim. Also line the bottom of the pan with parchment paper.

Dissolve the yeast in 4 tablespoons of the warm milk in a large bowl. Cover the bowl with a dish towel and leave in a warm place for 10 minutes until frothy. Stir in 1 cup of the flour and the remaining warm milk. Cover and allow to rise for 30 minutes.

Sift the remaining flour and salt onto the yeast mixture. Beat together the egg and egg yolks. Make a well in the flour and add the beaten eggs, sugar, and grated lemon and orange zest and mix to an elastic dough. Add more flour if necessary, but keep the dough quite soft.

Work in the softened butter. Cover and allow to rise for 2–4 hours until doubled in size. Meanwhile, chop the candied peel. Knock the dough down and knead in the fruit.

Place the dough in the pan, cut a cross on the top with a very sharp knife, cover, and allow to rise to 1 inch above the top of the pan. Bake in a preheated oven, 400°F, for 15 minutes then lower the heat to 350°F, Gas Mark 4 and bake for about 40 minutes until well risen and golden. Allow to cool in the pan for 10 minutes then transfer to a wire rack to cool completely.

For chocolate & nut panettone, follow the recipe above, replacing the candied peel and raisins with 5 oz roughly chopped semisweet chocolate and ²⁄₃ cup chopped toasted almonds or hazelnuts.

hazelnut chocolate ice cream

Serves **4**

Preparation time **10 minutes**, plus freezing

Cooking time **5 minutes**

1¼ cups **blanched hazelnuts**

1½ cups **hazelnut and chocolate spread**

1½ cups **evaporated milk**

Roughly crush the hazelnuts, then toast in a skillet over a low heat until lightly golden. Allow to cool.

Tip the spread into a bowl and stir in a quarter of the evaporated milk until you have a smooth mixture. Stir in the remaining evaporated milk, then fold in 1 cup toasted hazelnuts.

Churn in an ice-cream machine according to the manufacturer's instructions. Transfer to a plastic freezerproof container and freeze.

Alternatively, freeze the mixture in a shallow container or tray for 2 hours until half-frozen, then tip into a bowl and beat thoroughly to break up any ice crystals that may have formed. Return the mixture to the container and the freezer. Repeat the process at hourly intervals until the mixture is smooth and almost set. Finally, transfer the ice cream to a plastic freezerproof container and freeze until firm.

Remove the ice cream from the freezer 10 minutes before serving to soften slightly; it is best eaten within 48 hours. Sprinkle with the remaining hazelnuts and serve.

For speedy chunky chocolate ice cream, tip 3 cups good-quality chocolate ice cream into a bowl and allow to soften slightly. Lightly crush 3 oz chocolate wafer cookies and vigorously stir into the ice cream. Transfer to a plastic freezerproof container and freeze. Remove from the freezer and allow to soften slightly as above before serving.

sweet pastry ribbons

Makes about **35 ribbons**
Preparation time **25 minutes**
Cooking time **10 minutes**

1 **egg**
pinch of **salt**
2 tablespoons **vin santo** or
　sweet Marsala
4 drops of **vanilla extract**
1½ tablespoons **superfine**
　sugar
1½ cups **all-purpose flour**,
　plus extra for dusting
sunflower oil, for deep-frying
confectioners' sugar, for
　dusting

Put the egg, salt, vin santo or Marsala, vanilla extract, and superfine sugar in a food processor and pulse until combined. Add the flour and pulse again until you have a firm dough. Knead on a work surface for 2 minutes until smooth and elastic.

Set a pasta machine at the largest opening. Cut the dough into 3 rectangular pieces. Run 1 rectangle through the machine. Fold in half widthwise and run through again. Lower the setting by 1 notch and run the dough through again, then run once through each of the remaining settings. If the sheet becomes too long to handle, cut in half and run 1 half through at a time. If it becomes too sticky, dust with a little flour.

Lay the sheet on a surface dusted with flour and cover with a clean dish towel while you roll out the remaining dough. Use a sharp knife to cut the dough sheets into 1½ inch lengths.

Heat enough oil for deep-frying in a deep saucepan to 350–375°F, or until a cube of bread browns in 30 seconds. Add the ribbons, in batches, and cook for 30 seconds until golden all over. Drain on paper towels. Allow to cool completely, then generously dust with confectioners' sugar. The ribbons can be stored in an airtight container for up to 2 days.

For honey & cinnamon pastry ribbons, replace the superfine sugar with 1 tablespoon honey and use 1 teaspoon ground cinnamon instead of the vanilla extract. Prepare and cook as above.

watermelon & choc-chip sorbet

Serves **4–6**

Preparation time **20 minutes**,
plus chilling and freezing

Cooking time **5 minutes**

1½ lb **peeled watermelon**,
seeded and cubed

1¼ cups **superfine sugar**

8 tablespoons **lemon juice**

pink food coloring (optional)

1 **egg white**

¾ cup **chocolate chips**

Puree the watermelon in a food processor or blender. Add the sugar and process for 30 seconds.

Pour into a saucepan and bring slowly to a boil, stirring until the sugar has dissolved, then simmer for 1 minute. Remove from the heat, add the lemon juice, then allow to cool, adding a few drops of pink food coloring, if desired. Chill for at least 1 hour or overnight.

Use an ice-cream machine for the best results. Half-freeze the mixture according to the manufacturer's instructions, then lightly beat the egg white and add with the motor still running. Stir in the chocolate chips, then transfer to a plastic freezerproof container and freeze until firm.

Alternatively, freeze the mixture in a shallow freezer tray until frozen around the edges, then mash well with a fork. Beat the egg white until stiff in a bowl. Drop spoonfuls of the sorbet into the egg white while beating constantly with a hand-held electric mixer until the mixture is thick and foamy. Return to the freezer to firm up, then stir in the chocolate chips when almost frozen. Freeze until firm.

Transfer the sorbet to the refrigerator for 20 minutes before serving to soften. Serve with dessert cookies.

For watermelon & orange sorbet, omit the cinnamon and chocolate chips. Reduce the quantity of watermelon to 1 lb and process to a puree. Heat the sugar in a pan with 1 cup freshly squeezed orange juice, stirring until dissolved. Once cooled combine the watermelon, sweetened orange juice, and lemon juice. Freeze as above.

frozen bellini

Serves **4**
Preparation time **15 minutes**

1 ½ lb **ripe peaches**, pitted
½ cup **sweet sparkling wine**
juice of ½ **lemon**
1 tablespoon **confectioners'**
sugar, plus extra to taste
15 **ice cubes**

Put 1 lb of the peaches in a blender and blend to a puree. Transfer to a large bowl. Slice the remaining fruit, put in a separate bowl, and gently toss with the wine.

Whiz the lemon juice, confectioners' sugar, and ice cubes in the blender until the ice is well crushed—you may need to do this in stages to avoid overheating the blender.

Transfer the crushed ice mixture to the bowl with the fruit and stir well to combine thoroughly. Taste, adding more confectioners' sugar if necessary, and serve immediately, topped with the sliced fruit.

For cheat's strawberry & balsamic granita, replace the peaches with 4 cups strawberries, hulled. Puree 3 cups of the strawberries, then quarter the remaining strawberries and stir into 2 tablespoons aged balsamic vinegar, instead of the sparkling wine. Complete the recipe as above.

pistachio & pine nut biscotti

Makes **50**

Preparation time **20 minutes**, plus cooling

Cooking time **50 minutes– 1 hour**

1½ cups **shelled pistachio nuts**

2 tablespoons **pine nuts**

½ cup **unsalted butter**, softened, plus extra for greasing

1 cup **granulated sugar**

2 **eggs**, beaten

finely grated **zest** of 1 **lemon**

1 tablespoon **Amaretto di Saronno**

about 3 cups **all-purpose flour**, plus extra for dusting

1½ teaspoons **baking powder**

½ teaspoon **salt**

½ cup **coarse cornmeal**

Spread the pistachios and pine nuts out on a baking sheet and toast in a preheated oven, 325°F, for 5–10 minutes until golden. Remove the nuts and allow to cool but leave the oven on.

Beat the butter and sugar together in a large bowl until just mixed, then beat in the eggs, lemon zest, and Amaretto. Sift the flour, baking powder, and salt together into a separate bowl, then stir into the butter mixture with the cornmeal. Stir in the toasted pistachios and pine nuts.

Turn the dough out onto a floured work surface and knead until smooth, working in a little more flour if too sticky. Divide into quarters and roll each quarter into a sausage 2 inches long and ¾ inch thick. Flatten slightly. Place on 2 greased baking sheets and bake in the oven for about 35 minutes until just golden around the edges.

Allow to cool slightly, then cut on the diagonal into ½ inch thick slices. Place, cut-side down, on the baking sheets and bake for another 10–15 minutes until golden brown and crisp, being careful not to burn. Transfer to a wire rack to cool.

For almond & chocolate biscotti, replace the pistachios and pine nuts with 1½ cups blanched almonds and toast them as above. When adding the almonds to the cookie dough also include 4 oz roughly chopped semisweet chocolate. Shape and bake as above.

index

acknowledgments

Executive Editor Nicky Hill
Editor Kerenza Swift
Executive Art Editor Geoff Fennel
Designer Joanna MacGregor
Photographer Stephen Conroy
Home Economist Marina Filippelli
Props Stylist Liz Hippisley
Production Controller Carolin Stransky

Special photography: © Octopus Publishing Group Ltd/Stephen Conroy

Other photography: © Octopus Publishing Group Ltd